Public Speaking From Competent to Captivating

How to Be a Better Public Speaker and Overcome Your Speaking Anxiety, Fear and Overthinking

David E. Guggenheim, Ph.D.

Abyssal Scribe Publications LLC

APA Citation:

Guggenheim, D.E. (2023). *Public Speaking-From Competent to Captivating: How to Be a Better Public Speaker and Overcome Your Speaking Anxiety, Fear and Overthinking*. Abyssal Scribe Publications.

.

ISBN-13: 979-8-9894877-4-5 (Paperback) / 979-8-9894877-5-2 (Hardcover) / 979-8-9894877-1-4 (e-book) / 979-8-9894877-3-8 (Audiobook)

[v2.2]

"Be sincere. Be brief. Be seated."

Franklin D. Roosevelt

Contents

Preface

W hether you've given a show-and-tell presentation in fourth grade, a professional speech at a major health care conference, a training workshop on woodworking, a pep talk to your Little League team, a defense of your dissertation, a world history lesson to a class of high school juniors, a review of *The Woman in Me* by Brittany Spears to your book club, a report-out for your team in the conference room, etc., it means that you are a public speaker. That, in turn, means you've felt those butterflies, your quickened pulse, and perhaps a bead of sweat or two. You've looked your audience in the eye and felt their eyes on you.

Maybe you're a novice speaker seeking to master the fundamentals, or perhaps you're more experienced and have been speaking for years but feel that now's the time to take your speaking to the next level. Wherever you are in your journey, this book was written for you if you want to elevate your public speaking capabilities. I want to help you not only to be competent, but to elevate you to be a captivating speaker. What does "captivating" mean? In my experience, it's a speaker people will remember, when a speaker has made a strong, often emotional impact on their audience — no matter the subject — and someone who demonstrates confidence and warmly embraces their audience with respect.

It's impossible to omit nervousness and fear when it comes to discussing public speaking, and this book certainly addresses those topics. However, if you're looking for a book that is focused *primarily* on the psychology of fear, with the majority of its pages devoted to positive affirmations, breathing exercises, meditation or medications to take to calm your wits, this isn't your book. Those elements are certainly included (with the exception of medication recommendations), and addressing nervousness is a recurring and vital topic. However, I leave psychology to that field's professionals, and you'll find other books by such professionals that will no doubt be more helpful.

On the other hand, if you seek *specific, real-world advice* that goes deep, drawn from real experiences from a professional speaker's decades of experience, this is your book. I shatter persistent public speaking myths that are likely holding you back. I teach you how to build your speaking excellence and confidence, including how to write a compelling speech, connect with your audience with authenticity, and many other specific actions you can use to prepare and deliver an exceptional, impactful speech while reducing unnecessary stress and nervousness. In storytelling fashion, I endeavor to bring to life my advice through my real-world experiences

-- good, bad, bizarre, and comically embarrassing -- to guide you on your journey from merely competent to genuinely captivating.

Public speaking is an essential part of my job and something I am often paid to do, often traveling the world to do it. (See *About the Author* near the end of this book if you're interested in learning more about me.) In short, I'm an ocean conservation leader, ocean explorer, and university professor — not what most might expect a public speaking coach to be. So why read a public speaking book authored by, of all things, a marine biologist? Although our fields of specialty and messages we need to deliver might differ, we're more alike than different in our journeys of mastering public speaking. Each of us is trying to improve their public speaking skills in their field of specialization. I hope, like me, you see that as a strength of this book. We're on the same path, and as such, I think you can learn from my path through my real-world experience, not just theory. Taking nothing away from professional public speaking coaches, this book is about learning from the experiences of a peer, not a professional coach by trade. Learning from a peer is a perspective I personally find helpful when learning. I hope you do, too.

Selfishly, part of my motivation to write this book has come from years of sitting in the audience, attending countless meetings and conferences and enduring mediocre (and, at times, awful) presentations. My motivation also comes from witnessing presenters — some close colleagues — emotionally distressed during their turn at the podium. I am also motivated by my role as a professor, helping my students improve their public speaking skills. Finally, I was motivated to write this book from a personal passion, recognizing that there is a dire need to help people through something they dread yet know is essential to their success. I came to realize that there were important lessons there that I could share from my own experience.

Central to my experience and now philosophy is that much — if not *most* — of the nervousness in public speaking stems from underlying and often *unnecessary* stress. The good news is that if we invest the time and effort, this is stress that *we have control over*. Being prepared, crafting solid remarks, committing to practice, getting honest and constructive feedback, knowing your audience, knowing your venue, and anticipating problems all put you at a significant advantage over others in reducing needless stress and, in turn, nervousness.

Being prepared takes work. You must address a surprising number of seemingly minuscule details that can add up to create stress. But deal with these stressors in advance and you'll find yourself more confident as you begin your speech and gaze at your audience. Again, public speaking has an important psychological dimension, and this book does not ignore them. My emphasis is that dealing first with specific issues of preparation and technique can help enormously in reducing nervousness.

I do not overlook the fact that there are other factors that contribute to anxiety, some deeply personal and emotional. Some individuals may have challenges with nervousness and anxiety best handled by working with experts in those issues. However, I believe that the majority of you who face public speaking with dread haven't had the training that can mollify the surprising quantity of unnecessary nervousness that comes with public speaking. Such training can help you reach a new level of proficiency...to truly go from competent to captivating.

Public speaking is inescapably an emotional topic — for many, profoundly so. Therefore, I believe that providing advice without a human voice for readers to connect with would be a shortcoming. I hope you learn from — and occasionally laugh at — my anecdotes and experiences, coming from an actual human with real emotions. Again, I firmly believe a human touch is essential. So I've written this book in the first person. We're in this together, and we'll walk down this path together.

Introduction

My Sweaty Journey

I remember too well the day in my twenties when my world changed. I felt sweat pouring down the back of my neck, saturating my shirt under my suit. I incessantly mopped my brow with the back of my hand. I was about to give my part of a three-person presentation to a serious group of executives at a major utility company in Southern California. The large conference room was darkened, and I could barely make out the department head in the last row hidden in the shadows, arms crossed and radiating indifference, but more so, impatience. My heart pounded furiously. I was filled with butterflies as my turn in front of the group approached. I not only was fearful of speaking, but I even feared being fearful, in other words, losing my composure to the point of being unable to speak or remember my lines. My mouth was suddenly bone dry. I awaited my turn to speak.

I'm an extrovert and actually knew many of the members of the audience. But somehow, this was much different. There was intense pressure to do a good job and to have a significant new project approved. I was the youngest in the room. Who was I to speak to them with any authority? My mind was racing, and it was nearly impossible to slow it down. No positive affirmation in the world would pull me out of this. I knew I just had to focus on the substance of the presentation and do the best I could.

When my turn came up, I faced the audience and nervously began to speak. I choked on the early words I delivered, but then surprisingly, I discovered that the anticipation was worse than the actual speech. Once underway, I felt calmer, though still not exactly calm. I studied the faces of my audience and saw blank, indifferent stares. I imagined they could see my fear and feelings of inadequacy. Somehow I was able to get through my material, now so soaking wet beneath my suit jacket that I had to pull it in tightly to hide my saturated shirt. As relieved as I was that my talk wasn't a disaster, I knew that I left my audience informed, but certainly not inspired and probably not impressed. I received no questions and no feedback. I feared I left them with pity for the poor young speaker whose fear was all too evident.

My life changed that day because I eventually saw the positive in what I conveyed to the audience and I sensed that maybe my nervousness wasn't as visible to the audience as I imagined. I could see from that meeting how public speaking would be essential if I wanted to advance my career. But I had no idea how to proceed. I looked at other speakers that seemed "naturals" — calm, collected, funny and engaging. I figured good speakers were born that way and that there was nothing I could do — it was a skill that just didn't make it into my DNA and I would be doomed to a life of sweaty shirts and mediocre presentations.

Fast forward to present day. Trudging out of that presentation, I could never imagine that a few decades later, my future self would say that he loved public speaking, that he simply couldn't wait to take the stage and grab that microphone. Moreover, people loved to hear him speak, so much so that they would pay him thousands of dollars and fly him around the world to hear him, to places like Trinidad and Tobago, Israel, Canada, and to cities across the U.S. His audiences would leave inspired, at times in tears, occasionally mobbing him at the stage at the end of the talk. Some would ask for selfies or autographs from a speaker who is only a tiny bit famous, a stranger to most. At a recent talk for 100 students at a middle school in rural Virginia, young students had me autograph dirty napkins, Pokemon cards, and even their shoes! And most unbelievably, all of this was accomplished perspiration-free...for the most part, anyway.

As I reflect upon it, the public speaking journey I've made is something I never imagined and thought would be impossible. Are the butterflies still there? Yes — but they've made this journey with me. Instead of taunting me, "You're going to fail and look like a fool," they now challenge me, "Be on your game and inspire and wow your audience!" Even as a professor, the butterflies are there before each class. They tell me, "Be your very best, dedicate yourself to your students, and make a difference for them." More on your relationship with your butterflies later.

I want you to love public speaking as I do. It's an empowering, life-changing skill that opens up worlds of possibilities. A great speech can not only help you make important points, it can help you stand out from the masses of mediocre speakers, giving you credibility and the respect of your peers. It can lead to invitations to participate in conferences, projects, or even paid speaking engagements. For me it truly has indeed been life-changing.

Dragging you through the story of my sweat-drenched shirt was to show you that you and I may be more similar to you than you think. We're humans, with an extraordinary capacity to learn and improve ourselves. If I made this journey, you can, too. And I know that at some point along your journey, you'll move from dread to joy on your approach the podium.

An "Immersive" Approach

As one who now actually enjoys public speaking, I am much more conscious of how many people, including my students and peers, dread public speaking. It can induce a state of mind that lacks clarity, is virtually irrational, or, at worst, can even approach a panic-like state. While mental exercises can be helpful — and I discuss a few — my focus is on dealing with the *underlying stresses* that can cause such nervousness. From my experience, being prepared, gaining speaking experience and understanding the basic elements of a quality speech are three of the four secrets to quality public speaking. The fourth is one I strongly believe in: Respecting your audience. I show you how this philosophy translates into specific elements of your presentation — from timing to wording — and how as a result, your audience will be more engaged, enlightened, inspired, and appreciative.

I'm a true believer of "immersive education." Sitting in a classroom and learning the theory of, say, geology is one thing. Getting out in the field, dusty and dirty, and beholding those rock formations firsthand is a much more powerful and memorable experience. I've taught students ranging in age from 9 to nearly 90 using an immersive education approach and have seen the transformative impact it can have. It was immersive education that inspired me to pursue my career in conservation (more on that below) at the age of 15. While I'd love to take you up to the podium with me, I offer you the next best thing: As I convey in the *Preface*, I offer public speaking advice brought to life by a collection of my real-world experiences, including my tales of success and often comical tales of defeat. The speeches I've loved and those that I've absolutely abhorred. I've worked hard to convey my experiential education in public speaking to you real stories and real advice from a real professional public speaker. In so doing, I offer specific actions that you can take to guide you from writing a better speech, to nailing your time allotment, to connecting to your audience, along with a plethora of specific actions you can take to can remove a significant amount of stress from the equation, and many ways to improve your public speaking skills.

It surprises me how many myths persist about public speaking and how many of my friends and colleagues continue to believe in them. I, too, have fallen victim to them. The first step toward becoming a better public speaker is to shatter those myths. They're impediments and distractions, and some are just plain absurd. (For God's sake, please don't imagine your audience naked!) Together we'll get past those myths to focus on what's truly helpful and important.

I focus a great deal on preparing your remarks — it's where you'll spend most of your time. For a recent 40-minute speech in Philadelphia, I spent at least 8 hours preparing, and that was for a speech I had already delivered five times and for which I had already created a PowerPoint slide deck! In that example, I spent 12 times more time preparing my speech than giving it, and that applied only to developing my remarks and slides — it excluded working with the organizer, confirming logistics, choosing my wardrobe, setting up, etc. Good preparation has a wealth of benefits. It not only rewards your audience with a better presentation, it rewards you with confidence, knowing you've prepared well and knowing your material well.

What public speaking book would be complete without addressing fear and nervousness? In the following pages, I distinguish between stress and nervousness. Specifically, I have found that dealing with the many factors that create stress — some of them seemingly insignificant — has a dramatic effect in reducing nervousness. One of the most essential and empowering lessons I've ever learned is that there are certain aspects of the way I prepare for and perform my speeches that *I can control* and, when taken collectively, dramatically lessen the stress that fuels nervousness. Unburdened by such stress, you'll find yourself far less nervous and more empowered to take your public speaking to new levels.

Will you be able to give a speech without being nervous? I have given hundreds of addresses worldwide for decades, and I still get nervous, but I distinguish between "good nervous" and "bad nervous." Those little butterflies will always be fluttering about in your gut, but again, the message they bring will be much different — and much more positive — as you progress along your journey.

I teach you how your audience is not your enemy — in fact, they're part of your team. Your connection with them is everything. You're not talking at them — you're connecting with them. I discuss the importance of respecting your audience, not talking down to them or "dumbing it down." Of critical importance, I discuss the importance of avoiding rote recitation of facts. Like experiential education, you have opportunities to bring your material to life through storytelling, your personal experiences, emotion, and authenticity.

Technology and the use of visuals are widespread and can make — or break — a presentation. We are lucky to have powerful tools, like

PowerPoint, at our fingertips, but more often than not, we aren't taught how to use these tools correctly and more importantly, how best to incorporate visuals in our presentations. I provide guidance on using visuals, the importance of understanding the technology that powers them, and how to be sure that everything works smoothly on the big day.

Finally, in the wake of the pandemic has come the rise of the virtual conference and virtual speeches, the dynamics of which are dramatically different from in-person speeches. I discuss these dynamics and how to ensure your speech is compelling in a virtual environment. I also discuss the technology challenges — including the basics of setting up a home "studio" — so that your presence is professional.

Finally, it's an important goal to feel that you are a competent public speaker, one who can communicate clearly and confidently. I hope to take you beyond that, so your journey will take you from competent to captivating in time.

Four Steps to Effective Public Speaking

I guide you through four major steps to improving your public speaking abilities and confidence.

The four basic steps:

1. Overcoming the #1 Myth About Public Speaking and Dedicating Yourself to Training

2. Preparing Meticulously, Doing Your Research, Crafting Your Remarks, and Not Forgetting the "Little Things"

3. Practicing, Refining and Adapting

4. Speaking to, Connecting With, and Respecting Your Audience: Going From Competent to Captivating

At first glance, it may seem that there's a glaring omission, namely controlling nervousness, an essential priority for many trying to get to the next level in their mastery of public speaking. Don't worry — dealing with nervousness is, of course, part of this book. Still, as I said earlier, it's been my experience that you can dramatically reduce nervousness by reducing underlying stress, much of it seemingly trivial yet potent with pulse-raising effect. So when you take the stage knowing that your training, preparation, and practice have been thorough and that you're prepared for curve balls that may arise, you'll find yourself much more confident and, therefore, less nervous when delivering your remarks. In short, reduce stress and you'll reduce nervousness. Ultimately, these four elements lay the foundation for everything else you need to elevate your public speaking.

Part I

The Public Speaking Myth

"In the face of impossibility, remember that every skill was once unknown to someone. With determination and perseverance, you too can conquer the impossible."

Unknown

Chapter One

The Biggest Public Speaking Myth

"Myths are the shackles that bind our imagination and limit our potential."

Unknown

Nature or Nurture?

Exceptional public speakers who truly are "captivating" seem to possess innate talents that make them "naturals," exuding masterful oration, confidence and charisma. Nelson Mandela, Steve Jobs, Melinda Gates, Tony Robbins, Barack Obama, Oprah Winfrey, Winston Churchill, Martin Luther King Jr., Bill Clinton and John F. Kennedy among others stand out as those who seem somehow endowed with a birthright of extraordinary public speaking, out of the reach of the rest of us. It's a very common assumption that one must be born with the natural ability to be a great public speaker. I certainly subscribed to this myth, especially following my sweaty speech in Southern California. The skills of those master orators I admired seemed so far from my humble capabilities and it was tempting to simply give up on the idea that I, too, could master some of those skills. I likened it to basketball. On a good day I stand 5' 7", so I'm born at a height disadvantage to play pro basketball (not to mention my dismal playing abilities). Genetics do, of course, play a role in our abilities to master certain skills, and some speakers do seem to be born with some of the skills necessary to excel at public speaking.

But, being a scientist by training, I couldn't let this go and continued to analyze it. I became intrigued with speakers from the U.K. To an American ear, just hearing a Briton order pizza can seem like poetry, and it's not simply the accent which has a ring of sophistication to an American's ear. Britons have a reputation for polished and eloquent speaking skills, but surely all Britons aren't *born* great public speakers...are they? The formal education system in the U.K. has a long history and usually emphasizes oratory, debate, and rhetorical skills. Public speaking and elocution have historically played a significant role in British education, particularly in independent or private schools. Many British public speakers come across as expert, polished, and self-assured due to their emphasis on language and delivery.

In general, the U.S. educational system promotes more participation and engagement in public speaking. Debates, presentations, and extracurricular activities like public speaking lessons, speech festivals, and theatrical performances are all common opportunities for students in American schools. This encourages an emotional and affecting speaking style that stresses audience participation. These are generalizations, of course — public speaking instruction can differ in both systems with regard to effectiveness and quality.

The *Washington Post* reported on a 2014 report by Britain's Social Mobility and Child Poverty Commission, reporting:

> *"...British private schools still control politics and many top professions. One reason those people are so successful in public life is, of course, that their shared history gives them privileged networking connections. But they are also commonly very confident, fluent public speakers. They were not born that way. Their skills were developed through their school experience of debate, discussion groups and engaging in dialogs with their teachers. Although the term might not have been used, their education included oracy – skills in using spoken language – as well as literacy and numeracy."*
> (Mercer *et al.*, 2014.)

The title of an *Independent* article puts the British situation more bluntly: "*Old boy's club still dominates public life.*" (Grice, Andrew. August 28, 2014.)

The *Post* article goes on to make recommendations for U.S. schools based on this study:

> "*For the sake of social equality, all schools should teach children the public speaking skills they need for educational progress, for work and for full participation in democracy.*"

So this brings us to the mother of all myths that many of us may find discouraging and keep us from reaching our potential as an accomplished public speaker:

> **Myth**: **"Great public speakers are born, not made."**
>
> **Fact**: While some individuals may naturally possess certain qualities that contribute to effective public speaking, *public speaking skills can be learned, developed, and improved with practice and training.*

I believe this is the myth that holds most of us back. It certainly held me back in those early days. But, using the U.K. example, the public speakers we are most likely hear speaking in news broadcasts occupy positions of authority, and they have been the beneficiaries of extensive public speaking training, coming from inexperienced beginnings like the rest of us. Knowing I could become a better public speaker through training and practices was a powerful revelation and opened an important new chapter of my life. That chapter, however, would be a commitment to hard work, but in the end it paid off. I have had individuals approach me to tell me that I'm a "great public speaker" and in their eyes I can see that they're misled by the same myth — that I was born that way.

I would be remiss to omit the fact that there are some for whom public speaking may be a bridge too far. My retort to the "myth" is not absolute. For some, public speaking isn't about being nervous, it's about disabling, dark, traumatizing terror, and pushing one's self into public speaking could conceivably bring more harm than good. Again, I leave further discussion to counseling professionals, and leave it to you to determine where you might lie on that spectrum between being nervous and feeling traumatized. As I hope I illustrated in the *Introduction*, my own journey was one beginning with a potent dose of nervousness — to the point that my heart raced and sweat poured from my brow. But I did not feel traumatized. From what I've observed in my lifetime, and the growth of so many colleagues and students into confident, dynamic speakers, I think for most public speaking is a skill, like flying a plane, that may seem insurmountable at first, but with training and practice, can be mastered.

There are two related myths that also hold many back from realizing their true public speaking potential:

Myth: "You have to be an extrovert to be a successful public speaker."

Fact: I have read books and come across training programs based on this premise. I reject it. I believe it comes down to training, practice and feedback. Many introverts have excelled at public speaking. In fact, many I know have surprised themselves, finding another side of themselves quite comfortable on stage (while, interestingly, remaining introverted off-stage). The bottom line: Whether introvert or extrovert or virtually any personality type, anyone can improve and thrive in public speaking.

Myth: "In public speaking, charisma and stage presence are what make a speech successful."

Fact: Two of the most dismal talks I've ever endured were delivered by respected colleagues, each of whom exude charisma. But both failed to prepare clear, compelling remarks. The result was an unstructured, 45-minute meandering monologue. In other words,

they were "winging it," and their charisma and failed
to deliver a clear message, interact with the audience,
and convey information or ideas in an interesting
way, critical components of effective public speaking.

While charm and stage presence can improve a presentation's effi-
cacy, it won't carry the day. It's also important to say that as your
experience and confidence grow, you may find that your stage presence and charisma grow as well. They are qualities that contribute
to a good speech, but cannot carry a bad one.

In the end, this book's most crucial lesson may be to recognize and
dispel these and other myths. Doing so is what gave me the confidence and hope to become a better speaker. I pursued training,
and, well, it worked! Finally, it's also important to remember that
even those renowned public speakers mentioned earlier have had
to work on their craft to reach the level of proficiency they have
achieved.

Training to Be a Public Speaker

Unshackled by the "mother of all myths" about public speaking,
you may already feel a burst of newfound confidence and excitement and feel more ready to take your next step, freed of the
doubt that you need be born an excellent public speaker and the

confidence in knowing you can learn to be one. The first step is training.

In my twenties, I didn't even realize training for public speaking existed. I believed in the myth that there were natural-born speakers, so what would be the point of training for the rest of us?

Thankfully a friend directed me to Toastmasters International, an organization dedicated to public speaking, with more than 270,000 members and over 14,000 clubs worldwide. (Read more in *Beyond this Book* near the end of the book.) The organization supports its members in developing their public speaking abilities as well as other skills required for them to advance and become skilled public speakers. Each club member practices giving presentations while the other members analyze and offer feedback in a safe and nurturing environment. The roles are regularly reversed where one week you're delivering a speech, the next you're critiquing a speech. Both of these roles offer powerful learning experiences.

As my career developed and I delivered speeches more frequently, I came to understand how difficult it was to receive honest, unbiased feedback from my coworkers and friends because, out of politeness, they seldom provided criticism, even when it was helpful, and they lacked the skills to evaluate speeches. As a result, I grew to cherish Toastmasters' ability to offer impartial assessments and critiques.

Another element of Toastmasters training is the practice of impromptu speaking, that is, being assigned a topic that you must stand and speak on for a minute or two without any preparation. Though a bit nerve-wracking at first, those skills have proved invaluable, especially when conducting Q&A following a speech or perhaps finding yourself at the receiving end of a "Truth or Dare" question.

Understanding the guidelines of each talk and their stringent adherence to time limits (a green, yellow and red light system was used which you'll find is also used in a range of events) my confidence grew with each speech. Nevertheless, I felt that my audience could see right through that, through my rapidly beating heart and into my very soul to see that nervousness remained in my system. During the evaluation of one of my talks I was in disbelief and euphoric to hear my reviewers say, "You didn't look nervous at all." This was another critically important turning point in my speaking journey, a confidence booster on par with any other. It seemed incongruous that my exterior appearance and delivery somehow belied a relentless internal flood of adrenaline, rapidly beating heart and a mad desire to sprint for the exit. Yet I realized that at last I had reached a point — with practice, evaluation and feedback — where I had overcome an obstacle I couldn't imagine was possible.

Other Training Resources

Toastmasters International has chapters around the world is is probably the most well-known of public speaking clubs, but there are others. Rostrum is another public speaking organization, founded in Australia, with more than 100 clubs. A number of speaker's bureaus have training programs for speakers they feature and up-and-coming speakers.

In the U.S. you may find that in a university setting there may not be a course designed specifically to develop your individual public speaking skills but rather focus on applying communication skills to specific disciplines. This is true of the graduate course I teach. Each student is expected to lead a class discussion, participate in class and participate in a presentation of their major class project. While such classes can be quite valuable, they are not public speaking courses *per se*. Some courses are focused on public speaking although the courses tend to be more broad and, rather than titled "Public Speaking," they bear names like "Communications in Business." Drama, debate, communication, journalism are other resources for public speaking training. Such skills can carry over well into many forms of public speaking. (Again, see the chapter, *Beyond this Book* for additional information.)

With a growing trend toward online education has come an increasing number of online courses. Videos can provide virtual examples from which students can learn. Such courses could be especially beneficial if you're interested in improving virtual speaking, e.g., through Zoom, Teams, etc. However, as discussed in Part V, speaking online is quite different from speaking to a live audience for which there is no substitute for experiential education and that means standing and delivering before a live audience.

Training by no means ends with your training at a club or in a course. It also comes from ongoing learning, practice, feedback and feedback, discussed in the coming chapters.

Part II

Prepare and Practice

"By failing to prepare, you are preparing to fail."

Benjamin Franklin

Chapter Two

Crafting Your Remarks

"Writing is easy. All you have to do is cross out the wrong words."

Mark Twain

Invest the Time – Reap the Rewards

I confess that I am easily annoyed if I have to sit through a bad speech or presentation — and there are too many of them. Most of the bad speeches I've seen have fallen short due to a single factor: A lack of preparation. At the bottom of that barrel are speakers who speak extemporaneously but do so poorly, at times resulting at times in a ramble with no structure, no takeaway message, and at times are nakedly self-indulgent. I remember steaming in my seat, witnessing the perfect storm of hubris, lack of respect

for one's audience and leaving attendees who had so looked forward to seeing this well-known speaker leaving the auditorium
disappointed and let down. You may have seen disastrous toasts
at weddings and other events where the speaker had obviously
not considered their remarks ahead of time, fumbling through a
rambling, unstructured, and often awkward toast, quite possibly
fueled by the "confidence" sought in a glass of champagne.

I take the strong position that you must thoughtfully prepare *any*
speech, whether a dinner toast, a pep talk for your Little League
team, or a formal speech before the U.S. Congress. Preparation
means you know what your message is, you've created a structure
by which to deliver that message clearly and concisely, and have
considered your audience, the tone, etc. Sometimes this happens
in one's head in less than a minute, at other times in a mul-
ti-page speech requiring days. The bottom line is that "winging it"
without forethought can potentially be a recipe for disaster and
disrespectful to your audience. Experienced speakers may appear
to be winging it, but with practice, they have mastered crafting
quality, structured remarks in their heads in what would seem like
an impossibly short time. It's sometimes necessary to think on
one's feet when speaking...Q&A after a talk is a good example,
but usually there is some time to prepare. Recently I was part of
a panel discussion and delivered my formal remarks. I wanted to
raise a point during the discussion in response to what others were
saying. In that case, I grabbed a pen and a scrap of paper, created
a structured "mini speech" and delivered what I was told were

clear, coherent and convincing comments. Those three minutes of preparation meant everything.

Preparation of your remarks or presentation is, by far, where you will invest most of your time, and the more time you invest in prep, the greater the rewards. This is true even if you work with a speechwriter. Your investment of time is essential. There is a guideline commonly known as the "one hour per minute" rule, meaning that you'll invest an hour of preparation for each minute of your talk. That may seem like a jaw-dropping guideline. Could it take a solid work week of preparation (5 days x 8 hours/day) for a 40-minute speech? Yes. In my case — especially because I use many visuals in my presentations — I regularly exceed the one-hour-per-minute rule.

I am a bit of a perfectionist, and often I'm still preparing my PowerPoint as the announcement, "Flight attendants, prepare for landing" comes over the PA. If I'm speaking at a conference I'll often skip social events and lock myself in my hotel room to continue my prep. I've even scrawled notes just moments before taking the stage. Yes, my time management could be better, but it's the nature of writing and speaking that you develop new ideas and find ways to improve your remarks as you invest time in them. I'm also especially focused on preparation because I am regularly a keynote speaker, some of which I am paid for, so the stakes are high.

It's easy to underestimate the time required to prepare a speech, but consider the components: Defining the topic of your speech;

reviewing the guidelines from the event organizer(s); understanding who your audience is; ensuring your speech is authentic, engaging, and targeted at your audience; structuring, writing, editing, and rewriting your speech; conducting the research and fact-checking necessary to support your points or present new ideas; preparing visuals (a potentially very time-consuming process — more on that in Part IV); practicing and refining your speech; getting the timing right, etc. When you add it up, preparation time can be substantial. But *your investment of time will pay off enormously*, something you'll appreciate as you approach the podium, confident that you are in command of your material and ready to deliver a truly memorable speech.

Types of Speeches

The first step in writing your speech is, of course, understanding what type of speech you'll be giving and there are many. You'll also need to understand the audience you'll be addressing, which I discuss later in this chapter. Here are just a few examples of the many types of speeches among which may be one or more that you have given or will give:

Informational Speech: This is probably the most common type of speech where the speaker is called upon to educate their audience on a particular topic. This often includes offering one's opinion, presenting new information, etc. It can be as simple as a conference room report-out on a sales campaign in a conference room to providing global trends on hunger at a major meeting at the United Nations. I find giving an informational speech nearly identical to teaching in the classroom, though it tends to be less interactive, more formal, and of course, tailored to a different audience. What's key in an informational speech, as in just about any other speech, is to ensure strong research and fact-checking and to present the information compellingly, in other words, not devoid of emotion nor storytelling. The latter I discuss in detail later in this chapter.

Keynote Address: I feel fortunate to be called upon regularly to deliver keynote addresses. (I feel even more fortunate when paid to do so!) A keynote address is a prominent address presented at a conference or other major event. It is meant to frame the event by establishing the theme, tone, and central message(s) of the event. The keynote tends to be more dramatic, "bigger than life," sometimes presenting provocative questions that can serve to create a buzz, a challenge for the conference participants, or at times, just to piss everyone off. It is engaging, the goals being to generate excitement, thought-provoking ideas and questions. I've found that in many of the conferences to which I've been invited as a keynote speaker, there's more of an expectation to be entertained during the talk, whether that comes through humor, dazzling visuals, masterful storytelling, or surprising and compelling content.

Motivational Speech: In general, a motivational speech is meant to inspire and create a strong positive emotional response in your audience. While the lines are a bit fuzzy, I see a motivational speech and a keynote address as close cousins. Both contain similar elements, but in a motivational speech, the emotional content is stronger and more prominent. Through storytelling, personal anecdotes, and emotional appeals, the speaker encourages their audience to pursue their goals, overcome challenges or otherwise take action. I'd argue that in virtually any speech there's a dash of a motivational speech that is (or should be) part of the mix.

Persuasive Speech/Sales Presentation: Many of us are called upon to sell an idea, a proposal for a project, a concept, a course of action, or a point of view. Such presentations are very similar to informational speeches. They involve the use of compelling arguments, evidence based on scrupulous research, and rhetorical techniques to influence opinions or attitudes. Such speeches are especially common in business settings, i.e., the "sales pitch" to promote a product or service. (I have used this type of presentation often in my nonprofit work with foundations and individual donors to raise funds to support our work.) One must highlight the benefits of an action (donation or purchase) present (and hopefully inoculate against) potential objections, and ultimately persuade present or future clients, investors, or donors. I find such presentations among the most challenging as there is something important at stake beyond giving a good presentation which changes the dynamics of the presentation, your relationship with the audience which tends to be small.

Such speeches are often interrupted along the way with difficult, challenging questions which can, in turn, require you to alter your presentation in real-time. You may have worked tirelessly on a talk and accompanying slide deck that presents your case in a particular way, but along the way, it becomes clear that your audience wants you to take a different path through the material. This means you need to avoid being flustered and accommodate your audience by changing your path through the material — easier said than done since it can mean hunting and pecking through your written material and/or slide deck to achieve that. This underscores the importance of knowing your material well exceedingly well and doing your best to anticipate the questions from your audience and being prepared to take a different path.

Training or Demonstration Speech: If you're training or giving a demonstration of a product, skill, tool, concept, etc., you become the teacher. The challenge involves providing your students with a demonstration, step-by-step instructions. and often requires visual aids, props, or live demonstrations and hands-on engagement your students. Group discussions can also be an important tool in such training. I've observed that many such speeches are delivered by engineers or other technically-oriented professionals with limited communications training. Some have a tendency to overestimate the proficiency, experience, and knowledge of the audience. They may have difficulty communicating complex concepts and cling to jargon. And they may "over-explain" extraneous details about a product that may be exciting achievements and innovations from an engineer's perspective, but only of mild, if any, interest to the audience.

For training to be successful, four factors become especially significant: (1) You must inform your audience up front what they'll
be learning and what the end results will look like, i.e., the big
picture of the training and why it matters. For example, if you'll
be teaching how to assemble a piece of furniture, the audience
should first see what the end result should look like. Without the
vision of that end product in mind, the process of learning can be
undermined by the feeling among participants that each step of the
process is without context; (2) It's critical to know your audience's
skill level and, during the presentation, on the lookout for signs
that they don't understand or are having trouble.

In the early days of networked computer systems, we had to train
managers at a major electric utility company in California (yes,
the same one I mentioned in the *Introduction*) how to use a new
software system my team had developed. At the time, computers
(in this case, computer terminals connected to a central mainframe
computer) were typically only found on their administrative assis-
tants' desks for word processing and the like. For a manager to have
a computer on their desk was virtually unheard of. Some found the
very idea demeaning. This was a barrier we had never anticipated.
Now in front of a borderline hostile audience, we moved into the
training. The first step was to log in to one's account. Again, we
didn't anticipate that these managers had never learned to type.
For some, it appeared to be their first time in front of a computer.
In an agonizingly slow process, they would hunt and peck for the
correct letters. Many of the participants were quite burly, promot-

ed up the ranks from being linemen in the field. Their hands were huge, and they couldn't help but press two or more keys simultaneously. The fatal blow came when the participants couldn't enter their user IDs and passwords in less than one minute before the screen would automatically refresh. After a couple of tries, they threw up their hands and left the room. End of training.

It was a stark lesson to my colleagues and me that we had utterly failed to understand our audience before proceeding with the demo. How could we have avoided this disaster? Perhaps a pre-training with one or two managers to get their feedback and advice. And perhaps a chat with the IT department to see if they could keep those login screens from refreshing. Perhaps we would have ended up with the same result: We were too early to introduce this type of hands-on information system at a time when few knew how to use such technology and there remained stigmas regarding the very idea of a manager touching a keyboard at all. In the end, the point is obvious: Know your audience — their attitudes and their proficiencies — and if possible, work in advance with a small group to get feedback, advice, suggestions, and ideas.

As if that experience wasn't traumatizing enough, I led a training session for another system we had developed focused on managing information regarding wildlife species that the utility's activities could impact. Thankfully, in this case, the audience comprised more technically inclined individuals who were familiar with information systems, welcomed computers on their desks, and even knew how to type. It was an informal training of a dozen individuals. I sat in front of the terminal as they crowded around behind me. The manager asked me to pull up information on Bell's Vireo, an endangered songbird that depends on habitat in the company's area of operation. I entered "Bell's Vireo" in the query field, waited with anticipation, and to my horror, watched the system crash. I was perplexed and horrified — I thought we had tested the system thoroughly before the training. What could have possibly gone wrong? In the end, it was the innocuous apostrophe in the name of the bird that caused the crash. The presence of that character was not anticipated by the system — a programming error. The lesson is an obvious one: Whatever it is that you're demonstrating or training your audience to master, be absolutely certain that it functions flawlessly. This applies not only to software or physical items but also to training new techniques (perhaps yoga, meditation, or relaxation techniques). Be certain that they're tested and that you have practiced your training with a real-world group that, again, can provide valuable feedback.

Commemorative Speech: A commemorative speech honors and pays tribute to an individual, group, or event, often delivered on special occasions such as anniversaries, memorials, or historical commemorations. Such a speech may recognize achievement, include reflections on the history of an individual or organization, and anecdotes — from humorous to tragic. A successful commemorative speech contains strong, emotionally evocative content.

Ceremonial Speech: A close sibling of a commemorative speech, ceremonial speeches are delivered during formal occasions, such as graduations, weddings, funerals, and award ceremonies, aiming to celebrate or honor an event, person, or achievement. A ceremonial speech could be a simple wedding toast by the best man or a speech by the mayor, cutting the ribbon for a new baseball stadium. Ceremonial speeches and commemorative speeches are similar and their underlying components nearly identical. Unfortunately, such speeches can sometimes fall into the realm of perfunctory, nearly devoid of emotion.

I recently attended a university commencement for Master's students. As the students filed into the stadium, I found it a profoundly emotional experience, especially as I recognized several of my students in the procession. Sadly, that emotion was dashed as we endured a spiritless address by one of the university officials. The individual was reading the address, and the written words for them were beautiful and rich with emotional impact. But those words were read without emotion when they should have been "sung." The result was an uninspiring monotone delivery by a speaker who barely looked up from the paper they were reading from and showed no emotion on their face. Many of us tuned out. I was astonished at how such a monumental event with so much potential to move a stadium of thousands of onlookers fell flat.

On the other hand, at a prominent event in Manhattan just a few weeks prior, I witnessed an extraordinary ceremonial speech in a room of one thousand onlookers. Barely anyone knew the speaker but they will never forget him. The energy and emotion he invested in the delivery of his talk was jaw-dropping. "Oh my God, who is this guy? He's incredible!" is but one comment I overheard. The words he recited were beautiful (as were those written for the university official) but his delivery was profoundly powerful and emotional and truly brought those words to life. The audience was moved and brought to its feet. It is a speech I'll never forget.

Academic or Research Presentation: I'm trained as a scientist though these days I rarely give a purely academic/research presentation even though the material I present or teach is primarily related to science and research. I often say that I had to unlearn everything I had learned about academic/research presentations to communicate in my current career, which involves talking to a wide range of audiences, from the general public to students to members of Congress and even to other academics. (See Chapter 10.) In academic settings, researchers or scholars present their findings, studies, projects, etc. Such presentations typically follow a formulaic and structured format, including an introduction, methodology, results, and conclusions. The language used is typically dispassionate, and any conclusions are presented to avoid absolutes or certainty, full of equivocations. Scientists rarely present strong opinions, but this is changing. Scientists as advocates are still considered a risk for scientists who may be accused of losing their objectivity. Carl Sagan, the host of the original *Cosmos* television series, is said to have been ostracized by many of his peers for his role in popularizing science. Nevertheless, scientists can and do inject emotion into their presentations. And, believe it or not, we scientists do have a sense of humor. During the Census of Marine Life conducted in the 2000s, many new marine species were discovered over a decade of international ocean research, and many were dubbed with "interesting" names. In my presentations I like to use the example of a tube worm found deep in the waters of Spain. It sprouts a tangle of tentacles resembling dreadlocks from the top of its tubular body. It was named *Bobmarleya gadensis*, the Bob Marley worm.

These are just a few examples of the many different types of public speeches or presentations one might deliver. Each type requires a specific approach, structure, and delivery style. In the following sections, I break down the basic elements needed to craft a successful speech, how practice and get feedback, and how to anticipate and prepare for the unexpected. I think you'll find that there is great commonality among all of the above types of speeches, and by mastering the basic components, you'll find that you can master any of these types of speeches.

Know Your Audience

In the previous section, I gave a few examples of the importance of knowing your audience. This is important not only to the preparation phase of your speech but also to the delivery itself. For example, in Part III I discuss the importance of protocol, especially if dignitaries are present. Getting to know your audience in advance is crucial to ensure your remarks are relevant, timely, and exciting and crafting remarks with a central message that address-es the audience's expectations. Customizing your presentation to your audience may include the use of current, specific issues being faced by the organization you are addressing or perhaps important milestones that could be recognized. Such personalization of your remarks is appreciated and can add to your credibility. However, it is important to stress that you should take the time to get such information from your hosts and not take the shortcut of finding facts solely online. Your host can provide the most up-to-date information and coach you on what would be welcome for the au-dience to hear and what topics might generate discomfort. There are always politics that a speaker can be oblivious to, and saying the wrong thing could easily sink an otherwise quality presentation. Ensuring that your sources are credible and your information is up-to-date becomes essential in such situations.

Refining the content of my speech is often a back-and-forth process with the organizer, where I propose one or more topics and key points to which I receive feedback. You jointly explore ways to best tailor your speech to your audience during this process. The organizer may have some specific ideas in mind, and you may have others. Your host will also be able to shed light on other topics of interest, especially problems that they need to solve. Your role in addressing solutions will generate significant interest.

I try to reinforce parts of my talk that relate directly to the audi-ence's organization, coalition, conference, etc., by including images I've taken recently, sometimes on the same day. Even a group shot of some attendees can be met with appreciation and sometimes a welcome chuckle. It's little things like placing their logo alongside mine on a title slide. Be sure to let your audience see themselves in your presentation. While you're there, even if just for a few minutes, you're part of their organization.

As I learned the hard way and described in the prior section, it's critical to understand your audience's knowledge level and sophistication. While it's essential to ensure your audience understands what you are presenting, I have a strongly-held philosophy of never "dumbing things down," diluting content or using simplistic language that could come across as condescending. I believe we who speak are educators, and the burden is on us to develop material that may be challenging yet is expressed clearly and understandably. As president and CEO of the Conservancy of Southwest Florida, I asked that our docents use this strategy and develop new curriculum for our nature center where we educated our visitors, members of the general public. We conducted exit surveys and found that the satisfaction of the visitor experience went up significantly after this change. Learning new things is actually pleasurable and exciting with the right teacher. I actually use the same slide deck whether teaching kindergartners or undergraduates. They learn the same concepts, i.e., the material is not "dumbed down" or diluted for the younger students. The burden is on me to find the right approach and the right words by which to speak to each audience — more on this in Chapter 10.

Demographics play a role in understanding your audience: Age, gender, education level, occupation, and cultural background, all of which can influence their interests, values, and perspectives. A few years ago, I spoke to a gardening club in Colorado which was practically 100 percent women, most in their seventies and eighties. It was an excellent opportunity to discuss the role of women in environmental awareness and education.

At each event, in each venue, be sure to understand the range of attitudes and beliefs you may encounter in advance. It's an especially politically-charged world at present, and it is important to be vigilant about potential biases and preconceived notions related to your topics. Specific topics bring with them a seeming impossibility of having a rational discussion. In Chapter 6, I recount one memorable talk I gave about climate change to a room full of "climate deniers."

Disagreement with your audience on a particular topic is not necessarily a reason to excise it from your remarks and there can be pleasant surprises. In Orlando, Florida I spoke to a group of 300 real estate attorneys. For years I had lamented the number of golf courses in Florida and the missed opportunities to offer other types of amenities to homeowners, such as nature preserves and trails. Considering my audience, I had contemplated long and hard about making a provocative statement toward the end of my presentation and, in the end, decided to go ahead with it, saying (with a smile and a touch of levity), "I realize I'm probably committing heresy by saying this to a group of real estate attorneys, but don't we have *enough* golf courses in Florida?" I then discussed other alternatives. After the talk I was swarmed at the stage by attorneys who actually agreed with my remarks, and I'd like to think I planted a seed with them (no pun intended).

Finally, it is essential to consider your audience's cultural nuances and sensitivities. It may require asking questions of the event organizer(s), but be mindful of customs, traditions, and potential taboos before delivering your speech. Some language or examples may be offensive or misunderstood in their cultural context. In a diverse world, it is also important to consider inclusive wording, correct usage of gender pronouns, and other factors, some of which are rapidly emerging.

Your audience is the purpose you're on the stage. You'll hear me repeating the fact that respecting your audience is paramount, and that starts with understanding who they are, why they are there, and how you can help them.

It's About Writing

This isn't a book about writing — or is it? In fact, the same principles that apply to good writing apply to crafting a solid speech. So we must explore some fundamental principles of writing as they apply to writing a stellar speech. While some of this may seem obvious, writing remains a struggle for many. I consider it something of a window into the brain to understand how someone organizes and communicates information and I require a writing sample for candidates for positions I am hiring for. In a university setting, my students have found it helpful to review and strengthen some basic principles of writing for their assignments, so I have incorporated a mini-writing tutorial as part of my class. Yes, like public speaking, training and experience can make you a better writer.

Note that these guidelines were born of a science/policy class, but they apply universally. Above all is the need for a clear and crisp structure. No matter the quality of your content, if you don't handhold your audience through a structured presentation, that content can be lost in a soup of facts. I've had students pour as many facts as possible into an assigned paper, reciting from readings and my lectures. Their papers had virtually no structure and were close to incoherent without a clear central point or conclusion. (I've found such papers similar to modern-day debate competitions. If you haven't seen one, I suspect it's not at all what you might expect. Scoring points requires speaking as quickly as possible and reciting fact after fact. There's seemingly no structure, just incredibly fast-talking competitors with facts flying furiously.) While it's tempting to pack a plethora of points into your presentation, remember that structure matters, and so does editing your content, as we'll discuss shortly.

Making Your Case: Your introduction should include your principal point or position where you "state your case." The introduction should be clear, well-organized, and concise, setting the stage for the body of your talk where you'll support your case. (Your conclusion should tie back to your introduction, reminding your audience of your case and summarizing how you ultimately made your case.) Your introduction is crucial for capturing the audience's attention and setting the tone for your speech. It's also important to let your audience know where you'll be taking them during your talk, helping them understand and anticipate the structure of your address. In Part IV, I discuss how visuals can help you with this. Your introduction also provides an opportunity to establish your credibility. This is optional and depends in part on whether you were introduced (and choose to add or emphasize certain aspects of your introduction) or if you are introducing yourself, which is common, especially if you are a panelist. You may be introduced by name and affiliation, or you may not be introduced at all and asked to introduce yourself. I anticipate the latter and have bullet points written to guide me quickly through my bio, stressing the points that I believe are most relevant to my audience.

Myth or Fact?: "Begin your speech with a joke."

Discussion: It's helpful to start your speech with a "hook," i.e., a thought-provoking question, surprising fact, inspiring quote, or captivating story that helps you make your case up front. Whatever elements you choose to include may contain humor, which can be very well-received. However, there's a distinction between humor intrinsic to your content and telling a joke *per se* as an icebreaker. Yes, a joke can sometimes work, but I've watched speakers fumble over jokes that fell flat, some utterly irrelevant to the topic, all the while burning valuable time. Don't go there! Save it for the reception.

Supporting Your Case: The body of your speech will support your case. I advise my students to be clear if a point or position is their own opinion or one expressed in the source material that should be credited verbally or cited in written form in a visual. For example, in a recent speech, I said, "A 2018 study predicts that we will lose 70 to 90 percent of coral reefs by the end of the century." The slide on the screen showed the full citation of the study. I then said, "This is depressing, and it's easy to give up hope." Clearly, now I'm giving my own opinion. A compelling speech usually includes original thinking shaped by your own interpretation and expression of the source material, as opposed to a simple "cut and paste" recitation of the source material. (Sometimes, however, the goal of a speech can be essentially a literature review, in which case the "cut and paste" approach is appropriate.) As you make your case, you also have an opportunity to anticipate opposing points of view and inoculate for them in advance.

Stick the Landing: Too often, I've seen the conclusion of a talk as an afterthought, or worse, absent altogether, resulting in a weak or absent take-home message and a missed opportunity to make the speech genuinely memorable. The conclusion should summarize your main points and tie back to your introduction to reinforce your case or primary message. Ideally, you should find a way to punctuate your conclusion with a strong closing statement that leaves a lasting impression on the audience. Depending on your speech type, it may be a strong statement of your opinion, a call to action, a memorable quote, a thought-provoking question, or a compelling story.

Beware of "Absolutes": Passion is great, but unless you are directly citing a source, it's best to avoid statements that are "absolute," i.e., strong and unequivocal. It can be a delicate dance. Strong, provocative statements are often called for and can be influential in making a point. But it's essential to fuel those points with credible data. I stress this point because credibility is vital for one's presentation and reflects on the presenter personally. In many situations, it is often better to present a more nuanced statement. Some words I advised my students to avoid include "totally," "only," "completely," "absolutely," "literally," "unmitigated," among others.

Absolute: "The only way to solve the problem of climate change is to raise public awareness once and for all."

Nuanced: "A very important tool for solving the problem of climate change is raising public awareness."

Beware of "Colloquial" Words: A long list of words sounds overly colloquial. While not strictly forbidden, they should be used carefully and sparingly as they can come across as excessively informal and hyperbolic. When grading my students' papers, I will almost always get twitchy when I read words in an assignment such as "awesome," "amazing," "incredible," "frankly," etc. Such words also tend to be general or vague in their use. (If you use tools like Grammarly, you'll find they hate these words, too.) Contractions ("can't," "isn't") often do not have a place in a paper or a formal talk.

Beware of Jargon: I live in Washington, DC, the capital of the United States and capital of acronyms. Written reports and speeches teem with acronyms and insider jargon incomprehensible to outsiders. Try to be sparing in the use of jargon and acronyms. If you're talking about items manufactured by your company where you can expect everyone to understand the jargon and acronyms that's one thing. But beyond that, be careful. I remember more than one conference where an international audience looked befuddled when the speaker stated, "We really hit it out of the park." Baseball, in particular, is poorly understood in many countries outside of the U.S. and poorly understood by many living *inside* the U.S. Similarly, references to rugby by a resident of Australia may be met with blank stares by an American audience. Sports references are prevalent, but there are many other examples. Know your audience and write for them...and spare them too much jargon and too many acronyms. Also, consider how acronyms might translate in an international setting. At one meeting I attended, an Indian researcher presenting in the U.S. introduced a mathematical model with the unfortunate acronym of "ENEMA."

The Outline: Many of us were taught early on that writing a paper requires constructing a detailed outline. Only when that outline is complete do we begin to write and add the meat to the bones of the paper. In reality, the outline can be an important starting point, but its use — and attitudes toward it — vary widely among us. As noted in *Fiction Writing 101* (Bellever Books, 2022), those who strictly adhere to an outline "know what's coming up next" but "deny themselves the opportunity to surprise themselves" by allowing the material to evolve beyond the boundaries of the outline. Authors like Stephen King views outlining as "restrictive." Some fiction authors like to see where their characters may take them...a more organic process that may ultimately deviate significantly from the prescribed outline. I gravitate toward that approach, starting with a general outline but using an iterative approach to develop my speech and encouraging its organic growth, but only to a point. I have written little fiction but find the similarities striking between fiction and nonfiction when it comes to attitudes about outlines.

In addition, storytelling can play an important role in framing your speech, which we'll discuss more later. My preferred style for many addresses is taking my audience deep into a story that may appear to venture wildly off-topic. Eventually, that story line reconnects with the main topic, but the ride piqued curiosity and drew the audience into the talk. I remember a colleague who had enjoyed my talk about the Everglades, which I began with a story about a church in Russia, told me afterward, "I was wondering where you were going with that." Mission accomplished. So one's talk may be linear or, in my case, often "nonlinear" — the choice depends on the subject matter and your style. A sheriff's report to reporters about a local arson fire will likely be quite linear. On the other hand, a U.S. senator's presentation on a proposed bill may well take a nonlinear approach, using anecdotes to take the audience into a real-life situation that offers compelling reasons for the legislation.

There is no right or wrong answer regarding the use of an outline. The key is that your talk or presentation have structure: Make your case, back it up, and have a strong conclusion. How you navigate that material is something that should reflect your personal style, comfort and the type of speech or presentation you are giving. The other important takeaway is whether you're speaking or writing, those guidelines apply and preparing a memorable speech almost always means preparing with strong writing. This doesn't necessarily mean writing your speech word-for-word (though some conferences request a written transcript or abstract of your speech). Whether you read your words as a detailed script, deliver them from memory, paraphrase them, or extemporaneously use your own words and use your written words as a general guide, *structure matters.*

Your Scalpel is Your Best Friend

This is one of the most important sections of this book. You may also find it one of the most challenging — I know I do. Keeping a speech within your allotted time limit is one of the most common failures of delivered remarks. How many conferences have you attended that managed to stay on time? How often have you endured remarks that seemed to tortuously drone on and on? When crafting your speech, having your scalpel beside your pen is essential.

A quote I adore and often cite, especially in overly-long emails to colleagues, is: "If I had more time I would have written you a shorter letter." Exactly who penned the quote is uncertain — it has been attributed to Mark Twain, Benjamin Franklin, and Winston Churchill, among others. Its meaning is vital for writing, and especially for writing a speech. Brevity requires more effort and time than verbosity — distilling one's message into one that is clear and concise is work. It often requires cutting major sections of a report or speech that may be interesting but are not essential in supporting your principal point. Cutting parts of your talk that you were looking forward to presenting can be agonizing but is often necessary for a successful speech.

Why Your Scalpel Matters So Much

There are many reasons why keeping your speech succinct and within the allotted time limit matters so much, including the following:

- Ensuring that your speech stays within your allotted time limit can be an *enormous cause of stress*. For me, it's actually at the top of the list. Having the confidence that your speech will stay within the allotted time limit reduces the pressure to rush through your material and dramatically alleviates the accompanied stress. It's just like arriving at the airport early. The result will be a calmness enabling you to present your remarks while speaking at a natural, relaxed pace. It's not a pretty sight to see a speaker shocked to get the signal that they have two minutes left to wrap up, compensating by increasing the speed of their speech and rocketing through slides. Unfortunately, it's all too common. In the end the unprepared speaker's presentation becomes barely comprehensible and they invariably shortchange their conclusion.

- Keeping within your assigned time limit shows respect for your audience and the organizers. Both will very much appreciate this accomplishment.

- A shorter, more focused speech can more significantly impact the audience, conveying the essence of your message without unnecessary elaboration. It is also critical in helping you stay under your time limit.

- Shortening your speech forces you to identify its most critical points. Removing extraneous details allows you to deliver a more focused and impactful talk, allowing your audience to quickly and more fully understand the key takeaways. If you're making a persuasive speech or sales pitch, your persuasive power increases with a lean presentation that quickly gets to the point. This also allows for more Q&A and interaction with your audience.

- Making a smooth transition between different portions of your talk — the connective tissue, if you will — is important for keeping your audience with you on your journey. This may involve stressing certain items, using an interstitial slide (which we'll discuss later), or including an element all too rare from presentations: The dramatic pause. Saying nothing at all can be as important as talking. It can create a sense of drama and allow your audience to soak in the material you've presented. It's important to carve out time for this.

- Invariably there are unforeseen circumstances, including technical issues, venue issues, audience interruptions, other interactions, last-minute changes to your time allotment, and many other time-eating factors that can throw you off and eat into your time. (See some of my amusing anecdotes in Chapter 5.)

- Shortening your remarks can give you more time to engage with your audience, which can elevate a speech. Audience engagement can be as simple as pausing during an audience reaction, such as laughter, asking audience members questions, taking a poll, etc.

Why We Underestimate the Amount of Time to Deliver Our Remarks

When you do your first run-through of a talk, you might be shocked at how far over your time limit your talk is. This is almost always the case as I craft my remarks; sometimes, the overrun is significant. Why do we underestimate the time to deliver our remarks?

- At the top of the list is a failure to prepare, which includes a failure to use the scalpel. Without adequate preparation, a speaker may stray into tangents, speak without structure, or, in the example I gave earlier in this chapter, simply take the stage with no prepared remarks and "wing it."

- There is a natural tendency to underestimate the time required to deliver remarks in the transition from the written word to the spoken word, which requires understanding the formula guiding that transition (and lots of practice).

- Surprisingly, many speakers are unaware of the time allotted to them (until they arrive) or oblivious or obstinate when receiving desperate signals from timekeepers that they must stop talking. Again, they could have better prepared, respected the organizer and audience by wrapping up their remarks when asked to do so.

- At times speakers become overly attached to their prepared material, even if irrelevant or marginally helpful in supporting their point. However, that excess of information weakens rather than strengthens their presentation. The presenter may foray into the underlying engineering aspects of the device the students are being trained to operate, but the audience is there to learn how to operate the device, not the genius that created it.

- Things rarely go according to plan, and we can easily underestimate the time of our remarks if we fail to consider that.

How to Nail Your Time Allocation

The sections above have underscored the importance of the timing of your remarks and the challenges we can have in successfully keeping our remarks to the allocated time. Below are some pointers that should help.

- While it may seem obvious, be sure you know in advance from your point of contact the amount of time allocated for your talk. Write it down. You should also get in touch with your point of contact shortly before the event to confirm the time allocation. In some cases, I've had the allocated time changed but was not informed.

- Ask if there will be Q&A, and if so, will it be before or after your remarks? A crucial question is whether your time allocation includes Q&A or not. Also, you should ask whether Q&A will occur during or after your talk.

- Know the protocols in advance. Will there be a timekeeper? How will they inform you of the amount of time remaining? Holding up signs, hand signals, a simple look of panic on their face? Will they strictly enforce time limits? I sometimes encourage them to do so.

- Do some preliminary estimates. One method — if you've written your remarks — is to use the ratio of the written word to the time required in a speech. A common guideline — assuming a moderate speaking pace — is approximately 120-150 words to 1 minute of speaking time. This can be a useful starting point but should be taken as an estimate, not a precise figure. Time your speech for a slow, relaxed pace. It is almost always the case that we underestimate the time of our speech delivered this way as we rapidly read through the written version.

- As made clear above, you need to anticipate the unexpected and plan as best you can. Ask your organizer about possible scenarios. Prepare contingency plans (I list some below). But most important, build a buffer into your presentation time. I recommend a 10-20 percent buffer, which would translate to 2-4 minutes for a 20-minute speech.

- Adhere to the structure we discussed in the previous section: Make your case, support your case, and deliver a strong conclusion. Stay focused. Unnecessary digressions or stream-of-consciousness remarks can take you off course and burn time.

- As discussed above, use concise language: Choose your words carefully and opt for brevity. Be clear and direct in your communication.

- I always try to be the first speaker when I am one of several speakers, such as on a panel. Don't be afraid to ask the organizer or panel moderator in advance if that would be possible. Going first has the advantage of avoiding a sour and challenging scenario: On several occasions, the organizer has told speakers that they must cut the time of their remarks (just minutes before going on) because an earlier speaker had blown through their time limit. I've had this happen to me on more than one occasion when I was not the first speaker or near the top of the lineup, and it can be quite stressful to be modifying your remarks at the very last moment. If it is a panel discussion and you feel comfortable, encourage the moderator to be strict on time limits. Often they are not. Also, sometimes time allocations are cut at the last minute because another speaker has been added or for several other reasons. You need to be prepared for this scenario by planning for it. Prioritize the elements of your speech and know in advance what you'd cut.

- As discussed earlier, audience interaction is something that can be very positive but also time-consuming. It's up to you to be the enforcer and manage audience interaction. Sometimes audience members have a long speech they want to deliver, which can put you in the awkward position of having to cut them off. One method I've used is to interject and say, "You're making important points. Let's discuss those during Q&A or after the session." It usually works.

- We'll discuss visuals in Part IV, but it is essential to use them strategically in the context of time management. Be sure to keep the text on your visuals to a minimum for reasons to be discussed.

- Most important, practice your speech, refine it, and repeat the process several times. You not only improve your familiarity with the content, but it will generate new ideas and ensure the most accurate estimate of your talk's length.

This section has underscored the importance of having your scalpel beside your pen when crafting your speech. Knowing that your speech is the correct length and that you've prepared for contingencies, you'll find yourself more confident, relaxed, and less stressed (and therefore less nervous). You'll invariably give a better talk and show a better version of yourself. Keeping within your assigned time limit shows respect for your audience and the organizers. It may help get you invited back to speak in the future or recommended to others. Investing the time to perfect your timing is essential.

Remember, keeping a speech short does not mean sacrificing substance or impact. By focusing on your key message, prioritizing content, using concise language, and practicing effective time management, you can deliver a concise speech that engages your audience and leaves a lasting impression. And remember, you need to leave enough time not only for your introduction and body but also for your conclusion. Just like ending your remarks with a strong conclusion, timing is critically important. "Sticking the landing" not only means you've ended with a strong conclusion, but that you've done so on time!

Chapter Three

Practice, Refine, Repeat

"The more you practice, the better you get. The better
you get, the more you enjoy the game."

Michael Jordan

From the Written Word to the Spoken Word

You've crafted your remarks. Well done! Now it's time to change them. (Sorry.) Practice is vital for many reasons. One of its most important benefits is guiding the transition from the written word to the spoken word. Your written remarks will evolve as you practice verbally. Speaking words out loud processes the words differently in your brain, and often this leads to making modifications. Repetition helps you identify ways to improve your remarks, improvements that might otherwise have gone unnoticed. It can help you clarify your remarks, condense them, include items you left out, tailor your words for your audience, or reword portions to better align with your natural speech and style. Practicing is also about learning your pace and adjusting your speech accordingly. Usually, this means pulling out your trusty scalpel. When practicing by ourselves and speaking the words of our remarks, we tend to speak much faster than we would on the stage, so it's important to slow your speaking pace as you practice.

You may find that you're giving the same presentation or presentations multiple times. As your confidence builds, never skip the critical step of reviewing your presentation before delivering it. As your confidence improves, you may be tempted to skip this step. However, it's important to remember to incorporate new information, cut old information, and tailor your remarks for a different audience. Invariably, for the classes I teach, there is a barrage of new information that I must include in the lesson I had taught just the semester prior. Finally, if it's been some time since you last delivered your speech, you might see your work through new eyes and improve it. This happened to me when traveling by train from Washington, DC to New York. I realized my speech needed major surgery and was relieved to have booked the slow train.

Practice & Feedback

Practice and repetition are essential in improving your remarks in the transition from written word to spoken word, helping you refine your speech, a fundamental part of improving your delivery and confidence. Practice will help you familiarize yourself more deeply with your talk and memorize some or all of it, developing your style and technique, pacing (important), and, again, paying close attention to your time limit. Your talk will become easier, with smoother transitions and the more you practice. Most important, it will build your confidence and reduce your nervousness. You've practiced this. You know this. You've got this.

How Do You Practice and Get Feedback?

What are the best ways to practice? And how do you get honest, unbiased feedback? These are surprisingly tricky challenges. I discuss some myths below, but they're not absolute...they're nuanced. Each of us is different, and we need to discover which methods work best for ourselves.

Myth or Fact?: "Practice Your Speech in Front of a Mirror"

Discussion: If it works for you, great, but I've never been a fan of this commonly-touted method. The theory is that you can observe your body language, facial expressions, etc. while delivering speech. By seeing yourself in the mirror, you can adjust your nonverbal communication (gestures, eye contact, posture). In my experience the dynamics of speaking before a live audience — with the feedback, reaction, and engagement that go with it — are much different than speaking to an individual in the mirror — someone you know pretty well.

I feel self-conscious and critical when I observe myself giving a speech in the mirror so it actually undermines my confidence, but you may feel differently. That being said, I have found helpful observing in a mirror certain aspects of my physical appearance, especially my posture. Many of us, including me, tend to slouch and it can feel unnatural to stand tall. Here's where a mirror can help. If using a mirror, remember that you want your gestures to reflect the *real you* with authenticity and they should flow naturally. A variation of practicing in front of a mirror is recording yourself on video. While this may be an improvement on staring at yourself in a mirror, videos are most helpful when recorded during an actual speech in front of an audience, not alone in your kitchen. Again, it comes down to a matter of personal preference. If you find it helpful, by all means use that tool!

Myth or Fact?: "Practice Your Speech in Front of a Friend"

Discussion: The dynamics of speaking in front of an

individual — especially one you know — are vastly different than speaking in front of an audience.

Speaking in front of a friend or family member can actually be more challenging because, ironically, we tend to be more self-conscious and distracted. In front of a friend, your delivery will be different; you'll be more tempted to stop and perhaps say, "Wait, let me start over," or maybe you both may have a giggle or two. You're creating an unnatural "speaking" dynamic between the two of you. And it can be just plain awkward. Equally important, someone close to you often won't give you honest, critical feedback even if you need it. (This is also true of providing a "real" speech in front of an audience. It is exceedingly rare that anyone will give you honest feedback if it involves critique. Invariably it's either silence or "great job," whether that sentiment is sincere.) However, there is a case to be made for speaking in front of a friend or colleague whose input can be valuable. Just their very presence can be valuable. I've found that rather than standing up and pretending to give the actual speech, informally running through discrete sections can be very helpful for three reasons: (1) You have an opportunity for valuable input and feedback; (2) It can be helpful to experience your speech from the perspective of someone else; and (3) It can help you work out problems on your own. Perhaps you, like me, have had the experience of trying to solve a problem and seeking out a colleague. As you explain the issue, the answer might pop into your head without your colleague saying a word. Somehow we process information differently if we must explain it to someone else. So, rather than getting up and pretending you're giving the speech in front of your friend, I find it much more productive to sit down and read through my remarks, stop along the way, get feedback informally, and jointly work through challenges. You might stop and ask, "Does this sound right?" or "Do you think it might cause controversy if I say this?" This can be very productive. But beware: Even when adopting this technique, a close friend or family member may hold back on constructive criticism, and such feedback is what you need most.

What Works

So you might wonder, how do I practice if I don't practice in front of a mirror (or video) and if I don't practice in front of a friend? As mentioned above, working with a friend and working through your remarks informally can be quite valuable. But finding a friend or colleague — someone unbiased, unafraid to tell the truth, who will provide honest, constructive feedback, and who has the training and expertise to provide input properly — is essential. (By "properly," I mean in a constructive, not overly harsh way, engendering an environment where you feel comfortable and safe.) Such an individual is rare. Again, speaking clubs like Toastmasters International can provide you with such feedback and build your confidence.

Another alternative is to ask a colleague in the audience of your "real" speech to provide you with honest feedback. Just be sure to discuss this with them in advance, including specifically what type of feedback you're hoping they can provide. In the previous section, I discussed refining my talk on a train to New York. What I did on that train, and what works best for me, is to speak to myself in a low voice (or even just mouthing the words), reviewing my PowerPoint presentation or reading from my notes, all the while envisioning myself in front of the audience. This can be surprisingly effective. If you have a chance for a dress rehearsal in front of an audience, it's a great way to prepare because you can recreate many of the dynamics you'd experience in front of a real audience. Again, it's best if these are individuals who will give you honest feedback in a safe, constructive way. Friends and relatives aren't an ideal audience for this, as they'll try to be encouraging and may hold back on criticism. Finally, I find it very important to familiarize myself with the venue. I'll discuss this more in Chapter 4, but if you have a chance to see the venue in advance (the ballroom, conference room, golf course clubhouse or other location) where you'll be speaking, it can be of enormous help in preparing you, especially if you have the opportunity to hop up on stage and look out over the empty seats awaiting your audience's butts.

Timing

Again, I must stress timing. Whether staring into a mirror or mumbling to yourself on the train, when alone, we tend to speak faster than we would on the stage. Therefore it's important to pace yourself, slow down, and don't forget to include those dramatic pauses!

Part III

The Delivery

"Authenticity is magnetic. People are drawn to those who are genuine and true to themselves"

Robin Sharma

Chapter Four

Be a Boy Scout

"It has long been an axiom of mine that the little things are infinitely the most important."

Sherlock Holmes

Preparing for the 11th Hour

I n this section, we focus on delivering your speech. The good news is that the time you've invested in preparation now pays off in a set of remarks you can deliver with confidence and quality. We'll reprise some of the preparation elements in this section, illustrating how they then translate into your speaking experience.

But first, I'm afraid to say that your preparation isn't quite finished. As your speaking slot approaches, many little things can arise — often in the 11th hour — that can lead to unnecessary stress. Again, stress can be the underlying cause of much of our nervousness. Taking those stressors out of the equation — including the little things — will allow you to take that stage calmly and confidently, with unimpeded focus on your remarks.

The Boy Scout Motto

I was a Boy Scout, but I confess that I wasn't a big fan even though I did learn how to tie a damn fine clove hitch, sharpen a knife, and make a salad from dandelion leaves (yuck). In the end, however, the most valuable thing that the Boy Scouts imparted to me was the Boy Scout Motto: "*Be Prepared.*" In addition to your preparation and practice in the previous section, you must now be sure to "be prepared" for the home stretch before your speech. These are usually little things — many of a logistical nature — but they can contribute to unneeded stress and shift your concentration from your talk to resolving what may seem to be a minute detail yet somehow takes an hour or more to resolve. Below I list the most significant of these issues that I've had to deal with. However, every talk and every venue is different. Doing a run-through of your presentation is essential, concentrating this time on everything *except* the presentation. Visualize each step in the process and create a list of what needs to be done. Also, recognize that much depends on the organizers and whether they will handle such logistics for you. I've found that some do, some don't, and some didn't even think of half of the things you did. So "be prepared" in advance with your list and remove that unnecessary stress.

- **Always be Early**. Above all, being early removes a remarkable amount of stress from the equation. For out-of-town talks, I always try to arrive the day before I speak, be prepared for late flights, anticipate traffic, etc. (For a paid speech, I almost always include arrival the day prior as part of my contract.) Even if you're in your hotel room upstairs of the conference ballroom or break-out room, arrive at the venue early. I almost always eat breakfast, lunch, or dinner alone in my room before a talk rather than become involved in distracting conversations that can cause me to lose track of time. Many issues you would expect to be handily taken care of by the organizers and hotel staff can be overlooked, so it may well fall to you to get it right, and that takes time. If a session is already in progress before yours, it gives you a valuable opportunity to observe the room's dynamics. Finally, pad the amount of time you think you'll need to prepare. You'll often be buttonholed by someone in the hallway or the venue as people begin to arrive. So arrive early and be prepared.

- **Familiarize Yourself with the Venue.** Again, it can help reduce stress when you can see the room where you'll be speaking and, if lucky, stand on the stage and get a sense of what the dynamics and logistics will be. Familiarizing yourself with the venue can inform other questions you'll want to ask your organizer. At an opening keynote speech I gave in Ft. Myers, Florida, I found myself in a cavernous conference center. I wanted to see the venue where I'd speak the following day, but I was directed to the wrong ballroom, even asking for directions at every turn. In the end, it took nearly half an hour to locate the right room — which was locked. Thankfully, a hotel employee unlocked it for me. I couldn't imagine the stress that journey would have caused me the following morning and even introduced the possibility that I could have been late for my own speech.

- **Be Prepared for Last-Minute Changes**. Be prepared for last-minute room changes — you may not learn about such a change until you've talked with one of the organizers or a colleague. Similarly, the time of your talk may have changed. I've had some sessions run so late that my morning talk was postponed until after lunch, and I hadn't been informed. Worst of all, as discussed in the previous section, you may be asked to shorten your speech at the last minute.

- **Ask Questions, Lots of Them**: In the months or weeks since you were invited to speak, ask the organizer or your primary contact critical questions about your talk, such as what might have changed since, what logistics to be aware of, etc. It's been my experience that your contact doesn't always have the answers, so by asking them, you're putting them into action to find those answers. Such questions are simple, but some might require familiarity with the venue which your organizer may not yet have. Such questions are best asked a week or two before the event. Others at the event itself. I'm always sure to ask the following:

- *"How do I best contact you during the event? Where will you be?"* Be sure to get their mobile number if you don't already have it.

- *"I want to confirm that the length of my talk has not changed and is still x minutes plus y minutes for Q&A."* On several occasions, the allotted time of my talk changed, but I might not have known had I not checked.

- *"Who will be introducing me? Do you/they have the biographical information you need for my intro-duction? Should we review it?"* Your organizer, panel moderator, or other individual may introduce you, so be sure you know who it is, ideally weeks in advance, and confirm that shortly before your talk. In many cases the person who will be introducing you has left things to the last minute and cobbled your bio together from what they may have found on the Internet. I have been introduced on more than one occasion with outdated and/or incor-rect information. Your organizer will probably ask for your bio, but it's best to be proactive. I send a short, medium, and full-length bio well in advance. (I prefer to do the editing rather and have control over the information than leaving that task to the individual that will be introducing me.) Have a hard copy of that information with you and seek out the individual that will be introducing you in advance, and ideally, review their introduction. Finally, you should confirm that they will announce various logistical issues, such as explaining that there will be a Q&A session (or would that responsibility fall to you).

- *"Do I need to introduce the speaker following me?"* I once shared the podium with then-Vice President Al Gore and the Lieutenant Governor of Florida, Buddy McKay. I spoke after the Vice President, but none of the White House staff explained that I was supposed to introduce the Lieutenant Governor. As I stepped away from the podium and returned to my seat on the stage, an unpleasant staffer loudly whispered that I had forgotten to introduce McKay. It was too late and I was quite embarrassed. Had I taken the initiative to review the protocol with the organizers, I probably could have avoided what, at the time, seemed like a monumental disaster.

- *"Has the audience changed?"* You've prepared your talk for a particular audience. Has it changed? For example, often at large conferences, the organizers will sometimes invite school groups or others to sit in. It's great to recognize them and be able to tailor parts of your presentation to them. But you need to know in advance. If the dynamics of politics have changed because of the presence of representatives of government or a different group, be sure to be responsive. But don't let their politics throw you off your game to the point of diluting your message. I was once advised, shortly before my remarks in Corpus Christi, Texas, that local media would be present and that the word "conservation" was a word that was not appreciated and should be avoided. I responded by moving that word into a prominent position in the first paragraph of my presentation (and for good measure, sprinkled a few more occurrences throughout the talk). In the end you still have to be true to your message.

- *"Are there any changes that I need to make to my talk? Are there new issues that have evolved since we last spoke that should be addressed, i.e., incorporated into my remarks?"* Be sure what you'll be presenting isn't stale and addresses the most current issues that are of most concern to the audience.

- *"Will there be any dignitaries or other individuals in the room that I should recognize in my introductory remarks?"* This information can be quite dynamic, and you might not know with certainty who will be in attendance until the last minute. In the next section, we look at protocol and being sure you properly recognize dignitaries and others in the audience.

- *"**Can you provide me with the final schedule and when and where I'll be speaking**?"* I've found that sometimes the final schedule — undergoing last-minute surgery because of no-shows or other factors — is unavailable until the day of the conference, and the speakers are not always informed of changes until the last minute. It's best to be proactive and ask this in advance to the extent possible.

- *"**What's the dress code**?"* This one I find maddening. Seriously, what the hell is "smart business casual?" I find such categories insanely subjective. Ask your contact for some specific examples. And if you're a featured speaker at a conference, kick it up a notch. I was taught as a teenager to always try to dress better than those I would be meeting with, such as for a job interview. I've adopted this approach for other such meetings and most definitely in my public speaking gigs. It's a form of respect for your audience. It can be a great confidence booster to feel great in what you're wearing and know that you're showing a great version of yourself to your audience. Again, if you err, be sure to err on the formal side. This can seem strange at times — at a conference in Gainesville, Florida, I wore a suit and tie and looked out over a sea of Hawaiian shirts, linen pants, sandals, and flowing summer dresses. But if you're the speaker, it's not only appreciated, it's typically expected that you'll be dressed more "smartly" than your audience.

- *"Where should I be sitting before being called to the stage?"* If you're not told or you don't see a seat reserved for you, be sure to sit up front near the stage, or if on a panel, in the correct seat, typically arranged in the order that panelists will be speaking.

- *"Will there be a timekeeper?"* If so, what are the signals. Will they use a light system (for example, green, yellow, red); will someone hold up signs (for example, 10 minutes, 5 minutes, STOP!); hand gestures (for example, an outstretched hand showing five fingers, indicating five minutes, peace sign for two minutes, running a finger across the throat to stop. (Even if a timekeeper is present, I also rely on my own smartphone timer app. More on that in Chapters 5 and 8.)

- *"In what order will the panelists speak?"* When speaking on a panel, you'll speak to the panel moderator, ideally well in advance; this would be the opportunity to request to speak as the first or one of the early speakers (see Chapter 2). Again, there's nothing more maddening than to have a long-winded speaker at the beginning who eats into everyone's time, putting unnecessary time pressure on the rest of the panelists — at worst, causing them to have to shorten their presentations while on the stage.

- *"**What's Your Number? Can You Arrive Early**?"* If you're a panel moderator, be sure to get your panelists' mobile phone numbers, have them arrive early, and stick to your schedule, even if a panelist arrives late.

- *"**Will I be able to show visuals? Will I have a micro-phone**?"* See Part IV regarding logistics related to technology.

- *"**Will there be a spotlight on the speaker or is there a light on the podium to light me**?"* This can be important if the room is very dark for your slide presentation. You don't want to disappear into the darkness. Your face and gestures are part of the presentation but lighting of the speaker isn't always available. (Perhaps I'll add a portable selfie light to my "go bag.")

- *"**Is a riser available for the podium**?"* If you aren't tall (like me) I am practically lost behind the podium if it is especially tall. If this is your case ask your organizer if a riser is available. Being seen is important and a tall podium can rob you of your presence. (I try to escape standing behind a podium wherever possible — see the next chapter.)

- **Take Charge**. Don't rely on your organizer, moderator,

panel moderator, or venue staff to ensure everything is taken care of. In my experience I've found that many are inexperienced, untrained, and may be more nervous than you are while introducing you. I don't like to leave anything to chance. In fact, you may be in the position of educating them on how things should work, protocol, etc. For example, if there's to be Q&A you might want to supply the moderator with a suggested question *they* can ask.

• **Don't Stop Confirming.** In the 11th hour, a conference can take on a life of its own and sometimes run off the rails entirely. I've learned the hard way that confirming and re-confirming up to the day of the conference is critical. I've been burned twice by not doing so. On two separate occasions for different events, I worked for weeks putting together important videos. One was to be at the opening of a conference in Texas with the governor present. Unbeknownst to me, the host decided there wasn't enough time to show my video at the opening following the luncheon. I happened to walk into the room during the luncheon, and, to my horror, my video was playing with none of the accompanying stirring music. The video was washed out and barely visible with the ballroom lights at full intensity. No one was watching and I was crushed after putting so much time and effort into creating it. I had a similar experience in Washington, DC where the master of ceremonies hadn't been briefed about my other video. He told the audience, "Folks, there's a video; I don't know what it is, but why don't we just exit while it plays." Confirm and confirm again. Sometimes things go off the rails, but your intervention can make a big difference in rescuing your presentation.

As emphasized in the previous section, preparation goes a long way in reducing stress and, in turn, nervousness. Some of the details presented in this chapter seem insignificant. Even so, you can't leave them to chance. Once you've confirmed all of the "little things," you can take the stage confident that all of your preparation is behind you and that you know what to expect; you're ready for the unexpected (to the degree that you can); and you're familiar with the venue, confident that you're aware of any last-minute changes, informed of the logistics, protocol, and procedures. And you're satisfied that any technology, including your visuals, is locked and loaded and will perform flawlessly. And so will you!

Chapter Five

Delivery and Protocol

*"Advice from a tree: Stand tall and proud, Go out on
a limb, Remember your roots, Drink plenty of water,
Be content with your natural beauty, Enjoy the view."*

Ilan Shamir

Start Me Up

L ike my old '63 Dodge, most of my anxiety was at the onset,
putting my key in the ignition and hoping she cranked and
started. Hearing that engine turnover was euphoric — the anxiety
passed, and driving became a pleasure (well, as much fun as you
can get out of driving such a relic.) In the same way, it's natural
to feel anxiety in those last moments as your turn to speak approaches, whether you're doing a briefing to colleagues in a small

conference room, making a sales pitch to a group of executives in a more formal meeting, or making a keynote address in a grand ballroom. Some of the details will differ, but the basics are the same. This chapter will also underscore why padding your time is so critical. In the next chapter we'll discuss nervousness and why those butterflies aren't necessarily your enemy.

In the last chapter we discussed many of the questions you should be sure to ask your organizer, and in this chapter, we move ahead with implementing those factors as you speak.

- **Start Your Timer**: I do not recommend using your smartphone's built-in timer and recommend using a speech timer app instead (see technical details in Chapter 8). *Have the app open and ready before you are called to speak.* I usually start my timer while still seated to be sure I'm not fumbling with my smartphone on stage and typically add a minute or two to compensate for the introduction. You can place the phone on a table or even on the floor if there's no podium. In a conference room, I put it on the conference room table in front of me. And don't forget to put your phone into airplane mode. As discussed previously, be sure in advance you know the protocol and who your timekeeper is. Your timekeeper is often in the audience and may hold up cards with the remaining time. I actually find a human timekeeper distracting and prefer to rely on my timer. Timekeeping for some events/meetings is much less formal. The moderator may whisper to you, "Three more minutes," or point to their watch. If it looks like you're going over your time limit, and it feels appropriate, it can be a courtesy to the moderator to let them know you're finishing up and will do so within a minute. *Don't race through your closing remarks.* They need to be clear and robust — it's the message you're leaving with your audience. Remember, stick that landing.

- **Using a Teleprompter**: Some speakers prefer to use a teleprompter. If not provided by the venue, some rely on teleprompter apps that run on smartphones and tablets. Using a teleprompter app means your device needs to be at eye level (so you can read it and make eye contact with your audience), so you'll need a podium or stand. Be sure to set it up in advance!

- **Your Introduction**: If you're being introduced and if appropriate, shake hands with the person who introduced as you and proceed to the stage or front of the room. (Sometimes this protocol may take that person by surprise due to their inexperience in introducing speakers or using that particular protocol.) Approach the stage or front of the room with confidence and purpose while standing tall. For both the audience and me, it reinforces the fact that I'm the speaker. It also can help in speaking with more volume and authority.

- **On Stage**: We'll discuss more about the mechanics of

posture and delivery in the following sections, but the opening moments of your talk are important and, therefore, worthy of some discussion here. Projecting confidence at the onset is important, but how we do that is a matter of who we are and staying true to that. Regarding body mechanics and posture, standing tall and not slouching is essential.

- **Hands Out of Pockets**: Placing your hands in your pockets can undermine the perception of confidence by your audience while limiting the use of your hands in your talk.

- **At the Podium**: If you're speaking from a podium, again be sure that the light (if one exists) is turned on and illuminates your face. If the room is darkened to an extreme for your slide presentation to the point that you are lost in the darkness, the reading light can serve as a spotlight on your face to be sure your audience can see you. *Do not grasp the sides of the podium.* It creates an appearance of informality and can be distracting. Finally, if you are short and requested a riser, you may need to locate and position it if that hasn't been done.

- **Introduction Contingency**: As discussed in Part II, your organizer may fail to introduce you or provide a woefully incomplete introduction (such as simply your name and affiliation), an introduction based on ancient information gleaned from the Internet, or simply incorrect information. You may be asked to introduce yourself. This is an opportunity to introduce yourself how you'd like to be introduced, correct any errors and establish credibility. As we discussed in Part II, you're ready for this and have bullet points written to guide you quickly through the highlights of your bio, stressing those points that you believe are most relevant to your audience while being sure not to burn valuable time.

- **Thanks and Recognition**: Immediately after you are introduced, you should greet the audience, express thanks to the organizers, and recognize any dignitaries present (see below). It is important to ask your contact in advance who will be present that should be recognized, and you should ask again just before you start to be sure those on the list are actually present — often, they are not though it is common to recognize those in absentia.

- **Thanking the Organizers:** Following your introduction, greet the audience and thank the organizers for the opportunity to speak, acknowledging their hard work in making the event possible. Acknowledge any specific individuals or groups and recognize their contributions, as advised in advance by the organizer. Take the opportunity to recognize the importance and significance of the event and the vital work that everyone in the room is doing to advance the organization's goals or cause.

- **Recognizing Dignitaries**: Based on your prior conversation with the organizer, you should have a written list of the dignitaries present, their titles, and any other relevant information. It would be best to acknowledge their presence and possibly (briefly and concisely) acknowledge their accomplishments. You'll need to observe proper protocols in your introduction, so be sure to ask. When in doubt, err on the side of formality. For example, use titles such as "Mr.," "Ms.," "Doctor," etc. For members of Congress, it is expected to use "The Honorable" as a title. For foreign ambassadors and others, the term "His/Her Excellency" is sometimes used.

- **Provide Instructions**: I've experienced awkward situations where it fell upon me, the speaker, to provide logistical instructions because the person introducing me had failed to do so. Examples include reminding the audience to silence their phones...politely (e.g., "If you haven't already, I'd be grateful if you'd silence your phones.") You may need to remind the audience that there will be a Q&A period following your talk and that they should hold questions until then. As discussed in the previous section, try to talk with the person who will be introducing you in advance. Chances are that they will seek you out to get the introduction right.

Believe it or not, the hard part is now behind you. All that preparation has paid off; you're past the introduction and diving into your talk, which by now, you know intimately.

Standing and Delivering

Myth or Fact?: "Memorize Your Speech. Don't Use Notes"

Discussion: Whether to memorize your speech or read from notes depends on many factors, including the type of speech, the length of the address, and personal preference.

Toastmasters and other speaking groups strongly encourage memorization where possible. It's a valuable skill and helps significantly in helping you navigate your talk by remembering three or four key points you want to make. Those few points are anchors around which the rest of your speech flows naturally. There are also different types of notes that we touched on earlier. A verbatim speech is one extreme; a scrap of paper with a few key talking points is another. Typically I land in between unless I'm giving a talk I'm already very familiar with, in which case I speak from memory (often with a bit of help from PowerPoint, but only to cue me along the way). If I use notes, they typically include a sentence of each key point I want to cover and a few sentences I want to express literally. Your notes are not visible to the audience if you are speaking at a podium. However, suppose you are standing in front of a conference room or on stage without a podium. In that case, holding and reading from scraps of paper can appear awkward, distracting, and even unprofessional. In such cases, I'll hold a book or conference program with my notes placed on top. It's a cleaner look and makes it slightly less obvious that you're reading from notes. Always look up as you read — eye contact is essential, as is your own expression of emotion. *You're not there just to read a speech.* You're there as a human to share information with your colleagues. Embrace that humanity and express it. Equally important, never dump your speech into PowerPoint and read your slides. More on this in Part IV.

Be Yourself and Connect With Your Audience

Much of the difference between being "competent" and being "captivating" lies in your ability to be yourself and project your authenticity. It's also about making a strong connection with your audience. Eye contact with your audience is essential as is emotion and helping your audience feel what you feel about your subject. More on this in Chapter 9. Hand-in-hand with connecting with your audience is recognizing that they are not your enemy, they are on your side and part of your team — more in Chapter 6.

Escaping the Podium

If you have the choice of a portable hand-held microphone or a Lavaliere microphone (versus a fixed microphone on the podium), I encourage you to say "yes!" Being untethered from the podium allows you to move about the stage, engage different parts of the room, and enables you to be more animated — and human — as you speak. Being away from the protective armor of the podium can make you feel more vulnerable and exposed and may take some getting used to, so until you're ready, feel free to remain behind the podium. You may find that being at the podium is your preferred style, and that's just fine, but I encourage you to try a talk away from it, but double check first. As the opening speaker at a session of the Scottish Parliament, the A/V tech wired me up with a Lavaliere microphone, assuring me I could move anywhere. He was wrong. I was inaudible and had to return to the podium.

Posture and Movement

Don't overthink posture and movement — be yourself at all times. Given the advice to stand tall and not slouch, which we covered earlier, it's essential to "make it your own," i.e., not uncomfortably posed, something your audience may perceive. It can be helpful to emphasize points of your talk with various gestures and body movements. It can actually be a lot of fun. One of my presentations includes a photo of Mt. Everest, and I pantomime climbing up the mountain — it often gets a chuckle, or I might extend my arms with palms up to emphasize a "what the heck?" moment. But if it doesn't feel authentic to you, by all means, don't do it. Again, be yourself. Finally, don't cross your arms — it represents a defensive posture, which can distance you from your audience and undermine the connection you have worked hard to cultivate.

Speaking and Pacing

If possible, test your microphone in advance. I've had several instances where batteries in a wireless mike died mid-speech. Check to see if you'll have a microphone *at all*. When in doubt, I usually request one. If I don't need it, I was prepared just in case. Without a microphone you will need to project your voice. In *Seinfeld* parlance, I'm a "low talker," so projecting my voice can be challenging. Observe any cupped ears in the last rows of the audience to get a sense of whether you're being heard.

Stay focused. Don't feel obligated to react to unexpected noises, mobile phones ringing, loud conversations during your talk, etc. In the last section we discussed a polite way to instruct audience members who may interrupt to save questions for Q&A.

Use your voice to emphasize important points dramatically. For example, you can add a touch of drama by asking a rhetorical question like, "Can you *imagine* their surprise?" Such delivery helps ensure that you keep your audience engaged. Voice training is beyond the scope of this book, but many resources, including books, videos and apps exist. If you feel they would be helpful,

I encourage you to seek them out. Similarly, there are exercises to help excise "filler words" such as "um," "uh," and "y'know." (In Toastmasters we would count the number of "uh's" for each speaker. The individual with the most would be crowned "The Wizard of Uh's." It was all in good fun and helped us realize how many filler words we unconsciously used).

Remember, when crafting and timing your speech, you tuned it for a moderate pace of delivery, so be sure to stick to it. When we're nervous we tend to speed up our speaking pace, sometimes dramatically so. Again, as we discussed in Chapters 2 and 3, use dramatic pauses in your speech. Such pauses can be crucial to a talk, allowing the audience a few moments to process a critical point you've just presented. You'll also have some unexpected pauses, for example, following laughter or applause. It's instinctive to resume talking as soon as possible, but be sure to wait until you are confident you can be heard. With experience, this "sweet spot" can become instinctive.

If you read a quote or a passage from a book, the pacing should be much slower and considered. You generally want to deliver such remarks slowly and dramatically, which can strengthen the impact of what you're reading. You'll need to keep that in mind when timing your speech. During a recent book tour, I've been surprised at how much time reading sections of my book burns. I have compensated by editing and culling the passages I read.

Thinking on Your Feet and Adapting to Unexpected Situations

I've stressed "being prepared" and padding your speech with additional time because, invariably, you'll go off-script. Sometimes this will be due to your personal choice (you might suddenly flash on a short anecdote that illustrates your point) or something out of your control (a waiter drops a tray of plates and glasses, someone snores loudly, a fire alarm sounds, or a bird decides to offer commentary during your remarks — more on that below). Do not feel obligated to stop and comment on everything that happens out of your control. While you're speaking, it is, with rare exception, *you* who essentially plays the role of moderator as well as speaker. Take control as best you can, and have a strong filter when it comes to distractions, i.e., ignore inconsequential interruptions that may occur along the way.

Real-Time Fact Checking

Over the past couple of years, new dynamics have evolved in the classroom. My students have their laptops open and are Googling topics I'm presenting. In the process, they are fact-checking me in real time! Regarding a population of whales, a student corrected me by saying, "Professor, the number is actually 400 according to NOAA [National Oceanic and Atmospheric Administration]." I thanked her and politely said I'd correct the dated statistics in my slide. While some might consider this unnerving, I see real-time fact-checking as a positive development. It encourages interactivity and audience participation. Speakers and their audiences can learn from one another. You can sometimes weave such points into your talk with great impact. Humility goes a long way here. Don't be defensive...welcome their input and thank them. As we discussed earlier, if questions are to be taken at the end in a Q&A session, politely remind them. Protect your time allocation

Audience Interactions

The most common situations that arise that can throw you off your game come from audience interactions. You may be heckled, or individuals may shout out their (opposing) position on an issue. At other times, even if it is announced that a Q&A session is to follow the presentation, an audience member may be insistent and interrupt your talk. Nevertheless, some may raise their hands, at which point you have three choices: (1) Ignore them; (2) Remind them that there will be a Q&A session after the presentation; (3) Both remind them that there is a Q&A session but allow the question if they think it can't wait. Sometimes an individual may have a long speech they want to deliver, which puts you in the awkward position of having to cut them off. One method I've used is to interject and say, "You're making important points. Let's discuss those during Q&A or after the session." Again, respect your audience. They want to hear you, but they may also want to be heard.

Unforeseen and Occasionally Bizarre

Unfortunately, there are unforeseen circumstances, including technical issues, venue issues, audience interruptions, other interactions, last-minute changes to your time allotment, and many other factors that can throw you off and eat into your time. Most common in my case have been noise from passing emergency vehicles, helicopters, or ringing cell phones. I also encountered the occasional fire drill (some requiring the evacuation!) and the dreaded power outage. Be prepared to be without your visuals and possibly speaking in complete darkness.

There's no blanket way to deal with such situations except to maintain your composure, demonstrate grace under pressure, adapt, and be resilient. Here's where some padding your speech's time can help keep you on track should you encounter a bump in the road during your talk. Below are a few anecdotes of the train going off the rails during my talks that I hope you find both informative...and occasionally entertaining.

- Loud noise from an emergency vehicle, helicopter, or obnoxious cell phone ringtone can stop your presentation cold. Sometimes there are extremes. Once, giving an outdoor speech in Costa Rica, I was competing with a nearby parrot in someone's backyard, which perfectly imitated a shrieking, terrified woman. Someone said it sounded like someone was being murdered. Needless to say, it broke up the audience — and me — but took time from the presentation.

- Another comical situation was at a college in Sarasota, Florida. When I arrived and entered the lecture hall where my speech was scheduled, the *Rocky Horror Picture Show* was being screened, and the room was packed with screaming students. In fact, the hall had been triple booked. Resolving that situation was a herculean task (*Rocky Horror* fans don't like to be kicked out) and the scheduling mistake took an enormous bite out of my time.

- Another scenario is the time taken by your introduction. Your well-meaning host may take forever to introduce you. I have had hosts read my entire biography, stumbling over every big word — including my last name. Though this might nourish your ego, it also steals time from your presentation.

- As discussed earlier in this chapter, depending on protocol, you may need to recognize a long list of attendees in the room, including dignitaries, key figures in the hosting organization, and perhaps even the chef who prepared lunch.

- I flew from Washington, DC to a university in Mississippi to give a big Friday evening speech. When I arrived at the cavernous auditorium, only three students were present, and one was there just to do her homework. I went through with the presentation but sat on the edge of the stage, brought the lonely pair of students up to the front row, and made it more of a conversation. The same thing happened at a book signing event in Philadelphia. Three people showed up, and one of them was my cousin. I sat in the audience with them, and we had a conversation. In both cases, I thought I had done my job by being in touch with the organizers, but I probably could have done a better job of getting a sense of how (or if) the events were being publicized and how I could help (if possible) beyond the social media work I had already done.

- I flew to Michigan to speak at a middle school near Flint. Despite my assistant's ongoing communication with the school's administration, when I arrived none of the teaching staff had been informed that there was to be an assembly that day. A frantic scramble ensued, with the wide-eyed tech racing with the wheeled A/V equipment across the auditorium floor. Meanwhile, an announcement over the PA interrupted classes and asked everyone to report to the auditorium for an assembly. In the end, I traveled hundreds of miles to give a 30-minute talk, with no Q&A, and no classroom projects. Fortunately, I was able to adapt my talk which seemed to make an impact and was able to follow up remotely.

- At a school in Alaska, the morning announcements blared unexpectedly over the PA system in the middle of my talk, penalizing me more than five minutes of my presentation. The students and I shared the important moment when it was announced that today's lunch would be lasagna.

- To my horror, a colleague of mine with whom I was co-presenting deliberately "randomized" the order of the transparencies we were about to present (back in the days of overhead projectors). This was his style, not mine, and the stakes of this presentation were very high — a major funding proposal. This was early days for me in public speaking, and I stood in disbelief as my colleague began to speak extemporaneously, speaking about each slide in the random order in which they appeared. When my turn came up, my slides were hopelessly scrambled. I tried to mimic the confidence and smoothness of my colleague, but no doubt came up short. I tried to focus on my main points and weave them together with slides that didn't match what I was saying. My only advice in this situation is to stay on message and keep emphasizing your major points. (Miraculously, in the end our presentation was successful!)

- Co-speaking with a well-known underwater filmmaker, we took the stage at my former high school in Philadelphia. I was excited about this venue as an alumnus but quickly realized that the level of discipline had dramatically dropped in the years since I had graduated. That's a polite way of saying that it was a shit show. Students were talking loudly amongst themselves, giggling, and not paying attention at all. And then came the spitballs. I've spoken at hundreds of schools across the country. Occasionally, there were disciplinary issues, but nothing at this level. In such a case it's best to defer to the teachers in charge. We did. They failed. In the wise words of Steely Dan, "I'm never going back to my old school." In sharp contrast, just down the road that same day, we spoke at a Catholic parochial school. The nuns roamed the aisles, and the students were absolutely silent. Initially, it was refreshing compared to our prior experience, but then I found it difficult to speak to an audience where there was no feedback. They didn't laugh at my jokes (and, really, they were good jokes)! There were no "oohs" and "aahs" when we showed incredible underwater footage of whales and other creatures. I had the same experience at a parochial school in Wisconsin. But in the end, they loved the presentation — they just weren't allowed to speak during the program. Some even emailed me to tell me how much they enjoyed it. Yet it can throw you off your game when the audience doesn't react. Don't think the worst — every audience is different. They probably love every word.

- I had a somewhat similar experience when I was invited to speak at a university in Ohio. During my talk I observed the professor who had invited me, head slumped over into his palm with his eyes closed. "OMG," I thought, "the person who invited me is sleeping through my presentation!" His wife later informed me that he wasn't asleep at all — he best processes information from a speech by closing his eyes and listening intently. Phew.

- Before PowerPoint and Keynote were mainstream, our presentations were often done using carousel slide projectors. At a conference in Santa Barbara, I began my presentation and advanced the slides using the remote control. Without warning, the slide projector moved backward to my title slide. I then advanced two slides and, again, without warning, my slides moved backward, this time three slides. What ensued was a mathematical progression until the projector seemed to have a mind of its own. What we didn't realize is that the hotel had furnished remote controls using the same frequency to both our session and the one in the adjacent room, so we were controlling each others' slide projectors. Sometimes things go so wrong you just have to laugh...and most likely, your audience will likely be laughing along with you.

Sometimes you can be an exemplary Boy Scout and prepare and prepare and prepare. But in the end it's simply impossible to anticipate every scenario. Shit indeed happens. Anticipate what you can and do your best. Work the problem, maintain your composure and, as we'll discuss, remember that your audience is your on your side.

Leading the Conversation

Until now, we've focused on you as a speaker. In the last section, I made the point that while you're speaking, you are often playing the role of moderator of your audience, taking control of your audience. Of course, the head of your session may jump in, but part of your job as a speaker is to step up to the responsibility of being both speaker and moderator during your remarks.

In other cases, you may be invited to be the moderator of a particular session at a conference, to moderate a panel discussion, or to lead a class discussion. In almost all cases, this also involves making remarks of your own, so what we've learned about public speaking applies here. You may spend a few minutes introducing the discussion topic; introducing each speaker; interacting with the speakers, asking questions of them or commenting on their remarks; and providing final wrap-up remarks.

The skills of moderating *per se* include — but go beyond — public speaking proper, and it would take many pages to fully discuss the topic. Nevertheless, it is important to briefly discuss this important topic. In fact, I believe it is such an important skill that I require each of my graduate students to lead a 15-minute class discussion on a particular topic. They must introduce the topic and then lead and stimulate conversation, moderate it, and take charge along the way.

You'll find that what we have already reviewed about public speaking will be of great help in being a strong moderator. In particular, preparation and timing are of the utmost importance. Thinking on your feet — as we discussed in the prior section — becomes even more important given the dynamics of broader participation and unpredictable discourse. But now you must add a new skill set to the equation, simultaneously taking on the role of leader, diplomat, enforcer, and organizer. As a moderator, you need to facilitate a smoothly-running event, ensure that discussions stay on track and on time, and produce an end result that is a positive and engaging experience for audience and participants alike. Taking charge may feel awkward and intimidating. You may be introducing and moderating speakers famous in their fields for their vast accomplishments, celebrities, and others.

I have moderated many sessions, panels, conferences and classes and they don't always go the way you want, despite your best efforts. At a meeting in Cancún involving delegations from Cuba, México and the U.S., the opening statements devolved into political diatribes that I was powerless to stop despite repeated pleas to get us back on track. The entire first day was practically lost in a maelstrom of disjoint discord. My recourse was to have a sidebar with the Cuban delegation leader and ask that, if, by morning, he could provide me with a written list of his delegation's priorities that I could use to refocus our conversation. At breakfast, to my relief, he handed me a scrap of paper with six priorities. It saved the day and set the stage for a framework of international cooperation that endures today. The lesson: work offline and negotiate privately to regain control if you can.

Years earlier I experienced the same dynamic leading a meeting of 40 environmental groups in South Florida. In that case, incredibly, one of the groups was outside in the hallway conducting a press conference criticizing our dialogue. Like the Cancún meeting, not only was the session leader charged with facilitating the dialogue but also being a diplomat to bring order. It was also an awakening for me that there are some meeting participants whose goal is to be disruptive and push vigorously against consensus. I am not a psychiatrist, but it has often felt to me that a number of such individuals are focused more on themselves and a sense of self-importance rather than working as part of the group to solve a problem.

For more formal meetings, there are important tools guiding the rules of order of a discourse, the most widely-used in the United States being *Robert's Rules of Order*, often referred to as simply *Robert's Rules*, a manual of parliamentary procedure by U.S. Army officer Henry Martyn Robert, first published in 1876, and as of this writing in its 12th edition (Robert *et al.*, 2020). I have found that following parliamentary procedure can be a very effective tool in maintaining control of a meeting.

Below are some of the key elements that comprise the art of moderation. Again, this is a topic that requires many more pages, but my hope is that it will help you should you find yourself in the position of discussion leader or moderator.

- **Preparation**: You've already learned much of this in preparing your own remarks. Keep your remarks brief but be sure you have a strong introduction that clearly tells the audience (and reminds the panelists, students, group, etc.) of the goal of the discussion. If you're moderating a panel or session, be sure to have their presentations or abstracts well in advance. Study them carefully and interact with the presenters to fine-tune their remarks. Order your speakers in a logical progression that best tells the story.

- **Time Management**: Once again the scalpel is your friend. Allocate a speaking time to each participant, pad it (as you would do with your own remarks) and hold them to it. Let them know in advance that you'll be strict with timing. Also let them know how their speech will be timed and the signals that will be used. Cutting someone off is among the most unpleasant responsibilities of a moderator and yet one of the most important. The speaker will understand and forgive you and the audience will be grateful, though cutting off commentary by Meryl Streep is something few would dare. Discretion is involved as a particular speaker might be speaking on a topic so engaging and relevant that it is worth granting extra time, but don't be too generous. You might say, "Laura, we are over your time limit but we want to allow you to finish this point, so I can give you another two minutes to conclude this important thought." Perhaps you've endured watching a moderator fail to step up, allowing a discussion to degrade into an unstructured, undisciplined free-for-all. This is a disservice to all. To emphasize, the audience is greatly appreciative of a strong moderator who takes charge, provides structure and, of course, sticks the landing with a strong wrap-up/conclusion while doing so *on time*.

- **Thinking on Your Feet...Again**: Again, as discussed in the prior section, you'll need to be thinking on your feet, anticipating issues before they arise, and taking control.

- **Guide the Conversation**: The session title may say one thing, reinforced by your introduction, but that doesn't keep participants from straying off topic. Easier said than done; your job is to be sure each participant stays on topic. Be diplomatic, but you may need to interrupt and guide the speaker to bring their presentation back to the topic.

- **Diplomacy**: As a discussion leader or moderator, it is important to remain neutral and avoid expressing your own opinions. Your role is to facilitate the discussion. That being said, there are exceptions. For example, you might offer your opinion to provoke a more potent (and interesting) response. But in many situations, the more neutral you are, the more trusted you are by both the audience and participants. This applies to your opening and closing remarks. (Unfortunately, the moderator often omits closing remarks which should summarize what was said. Active listening and good contemporaneous notes are essential.) Various examples of diplomacy are also cited above, such as dealing with time and protocol and conflict. In case of disagreements or conflicts, it is critical to maintain your composure and refrain from taking sides while encouraging respectful discourse.

- **Encouraging Participation**: It's important to create a friendly, safe and inclusive environment where all participants feel comfortable sharing their thoughts and ideas, encouraging a range of perspectives. In such cases, it is important to allow everyone to be heard and be vigilant in preventing a few individuals from dominating the conversation while others to go unheard.

- **Q&A**: We have discussed Q&A in more than one section previously. Keep questions on topic and concise and you may announce that ahead of time. Do what you can to avoid those long-winded "questions" that are really comments in disguise. You may say, "Sorry to interrupt, but since we have limited time, please ask your question and we can discuss the other details later." In terms of logistics, it's common that only the speaker or moderator can hear the question, so in such cases be sure to repeat the question so everyone can hear it. For some discussions, you may have developed your own questions to kick off the Q&A session. Be brief and concise and be sure to allow time for the audience to ask questions after you.

Leading or moderating a discussion can be more challenging than public speaking alone, introducing new responsibilities and challenges. Ultimately, your audience will be grateful for the work you put in to preparation, organization and sticking to the time limit. They'll also appreciate your maintaining control of the meeting, as challenging as that can be at times. You're a public speaker after all, and that will help enormously taking this step into leading and moderating discussions. It's more difficult to rehearse this, but with practice, you'll find that it becomes easier. Don't worry — you've built confidence from learning, practicing and gaining experience at public speaking. You're in a better position than most to master being a leader and moderator.

Working With an Interpreter

Delivering a speech being translated by an interpreter presents unique challenges. Most people are accustomed to addressing an audience that speaks the same language and therefore are not accustomed to working with an interpreter. I have seen several speeches go awry, including by a city official accustomed to his smooth and flawless delivery, absolutely flummoxed working with an interpreter. If you are addressing an international audience and your speech will be translated by one or more interpreters, you must make several essential adaptations when crafting your speech, preparing to give your address, and delivering it.

First and foremost, it is vital to recognize professional interpreters as just that — professionals. It is wince-worthy to see interpreters occasionally treated as "the help," such as when, at a dinner party for international delegates, the host would snap her fingers, yelling, "Interpreter!" Professional interpreters often have advanced degrees and specialized training. Treat them as colleagues with the same respect and professionalism as any other professional.

Interpretation takes many forms. At the United Nations, professional interpreters from many countries occupy sound-proof booths and provide *simultaneous interpretation*, an intensely difficult skill to speak the translation into a microphone as the words are being said. Alternatively, a professional interpreter may provide *consecutive interpretation* in which the speaker speaks several sentences, stops, and the interpreter then speaks the translation. There are many other configurations that you may encounter. At some larger conferences, the audience can wear portable wired or wireless headsets, and the interpreters may sit in makeshift booths at the back of the room. Alternatively, there may be no booth at all. An interpreter may be seated at one end of the conference table, whispering into a microphone and transmitting to headsets at the table. In each of these situations, the interpreter's voice may be audible to the rest of the audience, and to the speaker, so it's important that both speaker and audience understand this in advance and are not distracted by it. One interpreter told me that in some situations where people had not been briefed, she was asked to be quiet by a member of the audience. When she was interpreting in a courtroom in the Midwestern U.S., the judge had never seen an interpreter and, mesmerized, called her the "magic talking lady."

Below is a list of some of the measures you can take to be sure that your interpreted speech goes smoothly:

- **Review Your Speech with Your Interpreter**: It is most appreciated by interpreters to be familiar in advance with the material you will be presenting, along with the terminology you'll be using. If possible, meet with your interpreter in advance to review. Alternatively, share your written remarks or PowerPoint slides. They will be most appreciative and able to deliver your translated remarks with better fidelity.

- **Cut the Length of Your Remarks**: Your scalpel returns to the scene when an interpreter is involved. Your pace will need to be slower when working with a simultaneous interpreter and will be even slower when working with a consecutive interpreter because you will have to stop to allow them to translate. Be prepared to cut the time of your remarks by 50 percent when working with a consecutive interpreter.

- **Go Slow, Be Clear**: You will need to speak more clearly and slowly. Avoid talking at a fast pace, but don't speak so slowly that it sounds unnatural. A moderate, comfortable pace is acceptable. Pacing may get some getting used to, but you'll quickly find your "sweet spot." Similarly, you'll also find your rhythm with a consecutive interpreter. Oh, and no need to shout. Your interpreter isn't deaf and comprehension doesn't improve with volume.

- **Don't Forget to Stop!**: Remember to stop after a two or three sentences when working with a consecutive interpreter to allow them to translate. Your interpreter must commit to memory what you are saying, so a long paragraph may lose detail and/or important points in translation.

- **Focus on Your Remarks**: You want to deliver excellent remarks, so focus on those. Don't lose focus thinking about the interpretation, and maintain eye contact with your audience, not your interpreter. That said, your interpreter may signal you to slow down or request clarification. Follow their instructions but remain focused.

- **Avoid Jargon**: We discussed the perils of jargon in Chapter 2. If you intend to use acronyms or other specialized words, ensure that your interpreter is prepared. You'll be addressing an international audience, so again, avoid sports and popular cultural references that others might not understand. "Home run" is a commonly understood baseball expression for an American, but not necessarily where baseball isn't played. While Elvis is probably widely known around the world, other pop culture references are not, so, for an American, avoiding references to the *Friends* and *I Love Lucy* TV series would be wise.

- **Check Your Interpreter's Credentials and Reputation**: If you're hiring an interpreter for a meeting, be sure that they come with good credentials and a strong reputation. Although I speak Spanish, it is not my first language, and at an important meeting I chose to have an interpreter present when speaking with a high-level official. The interpreter, chosen by a colleague and unknown to me, was terrible. He was inaudible, and even I could tell he was misinterpreting my words. I had to switch to Spanish for the rest of the meeting. Thankfully, the meeting ended successfully, but I learned an important lesson.

Speaking to an international audience is immensely fulfilling. Those talks are some of my most memorable speaking experiences. Your interpreter is your partner and instrumental to your success. Together you can communicate with your audience and make a memorable and enduring connection. (*And don't forget to thank your interpreter!*)

Chapter Six

Embracing Your Butterflies

"Speaking in public is easy. It's like riding a bike. Except the bike is on fire. And the ground is on fire. And everything is on fire because you're in hell."

Jerry Seinfeld

B y now I hope you've seen that there is a lot of work that goes into crafting, preparing and delivering your remarks, and that you've also learned that there are many pesky details along the way that you'll need to be on top of. But the payoff for all that effort and attention to detail is enormous — you'll set the stage (no pun intended) for a top-quality speech while dramatically reducing stress, and as I've repeated in each section, reducing nervousness starts with reducing underlying stress. That's one of the most important lessons I've learned and why it's a central focus of this book. In the past I recall my stressed-out inner voice yelling in my head just before I'd give a speech: "How much time do I have? Are my remarks too long? Is there Q&A? Can I control the volume of my videos? Do I have the full list of everyone to introduce and/or thank? Will all of my slides display properly? Am I dressed appropriately? Are there any parrots in the vicinity? Is my fly zipped?" Knowing you've addressed these issues in advance will allow you to take the stage with far less stress, reducing your nervousness and boosting your confidence. It's hard work, but all of these factors contribute to stress but as we learned in Chapter 4, are things that you can address in advance.

Good Butterflies, Bad Butterflies

At this point, you've admirably completed all of the hard preparatory work and you proudly stand in front of your audience ready to speak. Are the butterflies gone? I hope not. As I remember telling my daughter when she prepared to give a class presentation, "If you're not nervous, you're not alive." I've spoken hundreds of times. Are the butterflies still there? Yes — but they've made this journey with me. Instead of telling me, "You're going to fail and look like a fool," they now tell me, "Be on your game and inspire and wow your audience!" Even as a professor, the butterflies are there before each class. They tell me, "Be your very best, dedicate yourself to these students, and make a difference for them." It's a remarkable transition, but eventually you'll be able to embrace your butterflies rather than curse them. They communicate an important message and can impart enthusiasm, focus and energy.

Understanding Why You're Nervous

I've stressed preparation and reducing stress and how it will help reduce your nervousness...but it will likely not eliminate it. As mentioned in the *Preface*, there are, of course, other factors that contribute to anxiety and nervousness, some deeply personal and emotional. Public speaking is inescapably an emotional topic — for many, profoundly so, and the range of emotionally charged reasons that makes us nervous helps us understand why so many people dread the thought of speaking in front of an audience. Some of the factors contributing to the anxiety stemming from public speaking include:

- **Being the Center of Attention**: Early in my career, I was seated at a conference table with perhaps 10 others in Oakland, California to discuss a possible merger between the environmental consulting company I co-founded and another consulting firm. It was an important yet informal meeting, that is, we had discussion points but no formal script and no formal speeches among us. Just conversation. At one point I needed to make a point and jumped into the conversation. But suddenly feeling those feeling those 20 intense eyes upon me from around the conference table was unexpectedly overwhelming. I excused myself briefly to grab some water and regain my composure. In hindsight I had surprisingly little experience giving remarks around a conference table. My audience was close, their gaze more intensely felt. I was instantly very self-conscious and that feeling was interfering with the message I wanted to deliver. Ironically I would have felt much more comfortable addressing them from a podium in a convention hall. But it's an important lesson that you might be speaking to your audience in many a range of settings.

- **Fear of Being Judged, Rejected or Inadequate**: It's rare that everyone in your audience will fully agree with every word you say. Bringing new information to the table, even if it's controversial, is how we grow and how your words can contribute to change. Whether you're presenting a controversial topic in front of a large audience or a simple report-out at a small gathering of coworkers, it's natural — and helpful — to accept that there will be those who may reject your ideas. The anticipation of such rejection can trigger fear, but that fear is less based on the rejection of your message and more on being judged personally. In such cases it's important to focus on your message, not yourself (see *It's Not About You* below). Your message is what matters the most and needs your focus.

People may make judgments about you based on what you say, but, with notable exceptions in today's politically polarized world, audience members or co-workers will challenge the *content* of your message, and that gives you the opportunity to engage in a civilized discussion free of *ad hominem* attacks. There are exceptions, of course. When I was vice president of Ocean Conservancy, I attended a New England Fisheries Management Council meeting with our shark expert, Sonja Fordham. The issue at hand was dogfish, a small shark that, until recently, had been reviled as a "trash fish" but was now in demand and beginning to experience overfishing. Sonja delivered her testimony and immediately came under attack, including shouting from hostile fishers who were wide-eyed in disbelief that anyone could possibly give a shit about dogfish! Some of the fishers lobbed personal attacks. I was so impressed with how Sonja calmly, but firmly, responded to each of the questions and comments. From where I was sitting, the fact that Sonja maintained her composure and professionalism gave her voice more power and quieted the audience.

At times a disruptive audience member or meeting participant may seem to be attacking you personally, but in fact, attacking your message. At a meeting in Southwest Florida, I had an audience member throw a (thankfully small) copy of the U.S. Constitution at me, yelling, "You should read that!" I didn't take that as a personal attack, despite the fact that he did hurl a projectile at my head. He was furious about the message I was delivering opposing development in sensitive wetland areas.

I occasionally give talks to passengers aboard small cruise/expedition ships. During my lecture on the impacts of climate change on the oceans, I quickly realized I was speaking to a hostile audience of climate deniers. They asked hard questions, sometimes charged with emotion, but we ultimately had a spirited discourse. At the end, one of the attendees told me, "I don't agree with a thing you said but I respect the fact that you went ahead and presented the material."

In another example, I awaiting a flight in Dutch Harbor, Alaska, having just completed an expedition in the Bering Sea with Greenpeace and the National Oceanic and Atmospheric Administration to study deep-water corals that live thousands of feet below the surface. (They're spectacular!) The airport was fogged in, so a group of us waited and waited for the fog to lift. After some small talk, it soon became apparent that all of my fellow passengers had just come from a factory ship that was trawling for pollock. And here I was, fresh off a Greenpeace ship, soon becoming the center of attention. I explained that their trawl nets dragging across the bottom were scraping these important corals into their nets along with the fish they were hunting. I realized I was now actually giving a presentation, so out came the laptop with images of the corals we had descended 2,000 feet in a submersible to study and photograph. One of the crew said, "Yeh, I've seen those corals on our deck." I replied, "Right, and we're hoping to work with you to prevent that." By focusing our conversation on the message, it didn't become personal. That doesn't mean I didn't feel judged — of course, they saw me as a tree hugger — but focusing on the message made it possible to have a productive discourse. In the end, our flight was canceled, and we had to spend the night at a hotel. Some of us hung out at the bar, shared a beer and talked sports that night.

* **Lack of Confidence in One's Public Speaking Abilities**: If you've had little public speaking experience, it's quite natural to feel anxiety before your speech. As we've discussed, practice can make an enormous difference and build confidence. You needn't be flawless or a world-class orator. Forget about the amazing keynote speaker who drew a standing ovation a few minutes ago. You're prepared and your audience will clearly see and appreciate that. And as I was delighted to learn so many years ago, chances are good that your audience can't see your butterflies.

- **High Stakes**: It's one thing to give a briefing to the staff about the status of a new product. It's quite another to be making a presentation to a foundation for funding that can make or break a project for your organization. (I've made too many of those.) The additional pressure that is placed upon you is undeniable, and that can affect your delivery. In my experience, focusing on your message and being true to that message carries the day. Hand-in-hand is to observe your audience. If you're making an "ask" from a Venture Capitalist they will no doubt have questions for you. It may be appropriate for you to build short breaks into your presentation where you allow for limited Q&A. Such interaction is appreciated and keeps your audience engaged. The challenge is not allowing the conversation to be pulled off course. You now assume the role of a moderator and can gently remind your audience that it's time to move on.

- **Physical Reactions**: Each of us physically reacts differently to being nervous. As you read in the introduction, my body decided to sweat. (For the sweaters among us, I recommend having a neatly-folded cloth handkerchief at the ready. Pat gently.) You may blush. Other common symptoms include a quickened pulse, dry mouth, trembling, and increased breathing rate. While not precisely a physical reaction, as discussed in the last chapter, when nervous we tend to unconsciously increase our speaking tempo. For most of us, the way nervousness physically manifests itself is not a pleasant feeling. In the moment, it feels debilitating. In some cases, it can make us feel panicky. Some of these physical reactions we can ameliorate, but some may be difficult to control. I discuss below ways to deal with nervousness, including the physical symptoms that we must all surmount.

Be a Scuba Diver

The combination of one or all of the above factors contributing to nervousness can at best be a nuisance and at worst interfere with our ability to deliver our remarks, perhaps clouding our focus or in rare cases contribute to a feeling of being panicky which can make it hard to think clearly.

Enter the scuba diver. (Please indulge me – I am a marine scientist after all.) I've been a scuba diver since I was 14 and it has taught me many life lessons, some of which apply to public speaking. Training as a scuba diver teaches us that the number one danger in diving is panic. In such a confused, anxiety-fueled state, one's behavior can be irrational and life-threatening. Therefore, much of scuba training focuses on preventing panic. A foundational part of that process lies in being well-trained, familiar with your equipment and comfortable in the water, so if something goes awry, you're prepared.

The training I had during my teens always focused at its core on staying calm and rational under stress. Different instructors had different ways of giving us our "stress test." In hindsight, what I went through seems comically sadistic. Most scuba divers go through an exercise called "Ditch and Don." You descend to the bottom, remove everything but your Speedos, "ditch" your equipment on the bottom, shut off the air, and return to the surface where you tread water for a few minutes. You'd then swim back to the bottom, locate and "don" your equipment, clear your mask and return to the surface. It can be a stressful training exercise but is exceptional in helping you familiarize yourself with your equipment while helping you build confidence under stress, key to avoiding panic.

In my case, my fellow students and I endured "Ditch and Don *With Harassment*," as it was called, that allowed our instructors to subject us to their dark side. We would ditch our equipment upon an underwater wooden platform at a depth of roughly twenty feet, return to the surface, and tread water while our instructors disappeared below the surface to begin their devilish deeds. After twenty minutes they returned to the surface and gave the signal. When I arrived at the bottom it was difficult to comprehend what I was seeing since I wasn't wearing a mask. I didn't see my tank at all.

As we were taught, I had to tame my noisy brain that was intimidated by the enormity of the task I faced by slowing things down, analyzing the issues I was facing, prioritizing them, and dealing with them *one by one*....and doing so calmly and methodically. Breathing, of course, was at the top of the priority list. I was happy to find the mouthpiece of my regulator on the platform, but the hose snaked downward through one of the 3-inch spaces between the wooden slats and disappeared beneath the platform. I tried to draw a breath — nothing. The air was turned off. So I ducked beneath the platform, located my tank, turned on the air, returned to my regulator atop the platform and thus solved the first challenge on my list. Well, sort of. I'd still have to figure out how to get my tank free, but that could wait.

Next on the list was my mask, without which everything was a blur. Thankfully I found it nearby, but when I tried to pull it toward me, it pulled back. My considerate instructors had removed the strap, and then reattached it, looping it through the slats in the platform. Sinister! So I slowly and calmly removed the strap, pulled it free from the platform, reattached it to the mask, placed the mask on my face and cleared it of water. I could see! But what I saw was definitely not what I wanted to see. One of the instructors appeared in front of me and promptly ripped the mask from my face and tossed it out of reach across the platform. If you haven't guessed, this was the "harassment" part of the exercise. The rest of the exercise was annoying but easy. I had my air and that's really all that mattered. The instructors continued to invent other unpleasantries for the next 20 minutes until I finally had all of my gear on and they allowed me to return to the surface. In the end, the lessons I've taken away from scuba diving apply to many other aspects of life, and that most definitely includes public speaking. Three are especially relevant:

- **Slow Things Down**: When I teach new scuba divers, I always say that there's virtually nothing you need to do quickly, so slow it down and be calm, even if a malicious instructor keeps pulling your mask off. The same goes if you're at the podium. If you're under stress, do your best to slow everything down. This is often easier said than done because our perception of time at the podium tends to be distorted. A pause of just a couple of seconds can seem like minutes, so we tend to agonize about any sort of delay. Don't sweat it — your audience will probably not notice a thing. You'll feel calmer and better able to focus. Take a breath (a priority whether you're above or below the water). More on breathing below.

- **Deal With Stressors One by One**: Finding yourself in a whirlwind of stressors enveloping you can be paralyzing and disorienting. Slowing things down allows you to be better able to clearly understand, one by one, each of the issues causing your stress and in sequence deal with the ones that you can control in the moment. As for the rest, do your best to acknowledge them but put them aside, the priority being to focus on the remarks prepared and practiced well. It's not always easy, but like dealing with "Ditch and Don With Harassment," dealing with issues one by one is empowering and can help keep you calm and focused.

In Cuba I was delivering an important talk, but unexpectedly became stressed about the fact that certain videos in my presentation were not playing correctly on the outdated equipment being used by the host. Then, to my dismay, just a couple of minutes into my talk, a leading government official, for whom the presentation was a priority, received a call on her mobile phone and left the room for the duration. Finally, I was preoccupied with the fact that, as the last of several speakers, a number of the important points I was to make had already been made by the panelists who went before me. The combination of these unanticipated factors swirled in my head. I took a breath and did my best to quickly sort through each of the elements one by one. Most important, I remembered that I needed to do my best to engage with my audience and focus on my message. After a few sentences I was able to shake off most of the unexpected stress.

- **Be Prepared**: Reprising the Boy Scout motto, "Ditch and Don" would be impossible without adequate familiarity with one's equipment and practice. For the public speaker, having prepared and having practiced will build great comfort and confidence when you speak. As you dissect your stress into each of the individual stressors, you'll be better able to use that training and experience to deal with them...slowly...one-by-one.

More on Managing Nervousness

I believe that for the majority, being prepared, having practiced, slowing things down, and addressing stressors one by one are essential elements to help reduce the stress, effective in reducing nervousness to the point that it's manageable, allowing you to take the stage and deliver a great, memorable talk, reaching a new level of proficiency, on your way to truly go from competent to captivating.

Beyond that, there are exercises and tools focused on your physical and mental state that can be effective at reducing nervousness. As mentioned in the *Preface*, I do not overlook the fact that there are other factors that contribute to anxiety, some deeply personal and emotional. Some of you may have challenges with nervousness and anxiety best handled by working with specialists or consulting other books on that topic. Below I discuss below some additional tools that can be effective.

- **Breathing:** I find the classic "deep breath in through the nose and out through the mouth" surprisingly effective. If you do it slowly, it also helps you with the "slow things down" mindset. There are many other types of breathing exercises designed to help you reduce stress and anxiety and you can find good examples from yoga, mindfulness exercises and guided meditation techniques. Others include deep belly breathing (also known as breathing from the diaphragm); timed breathing (such as box/square breathing, 4-7-8 breathing (also known as square breathing); counted breathing and other variations of timing and holding of your breath; alternative nostril breathing (is pretty much what it sounds like). There are a variety of sources to learn more about breathing exercises. Breathing exercises are easy. You need no special equipment and you can do it anywhere. I usually sneak in a couple of deep breaths as I'm being introduced.

- **Exercise**: A good, strenuous workout before your talk can help you clear your noisy mind and fill your bloodstream with endorphins. I find it one of the best natural ways of dealing with stressful situations of any kind. At work or conferences, sneaking in a workout can be challenging. A short walk can be a nice alternative.

- **Relaxation Music, Guided Relaxation and Apps**: The number of YouTube videos focused on guided meditation and relaxation has grown, along with a variety of smartphone apps. Typically a human voice guides you through relaxation techniques. Such content often includes breathing exercises. Alternatively, soothing music can work to relax you as well. Just be sure you don't nod off before you're called to the podium.

- **AC/DC:** At the other end of the spectrum, I have a

friend who finds more relaxation from an especially loud rendition of AC/DC's "Highway to Hell." While it's not usually my first choice before a talk (though it was great for pumping me up before a sports competition), it can be a great stress buster and confidence builder.

• **Visualize Your Success**: I've been pleasantly surprised at how simply imagining myself on stage and successfully making a great presentation can help build my confidence. I typically do this shortly before I take the stage and it puts a confident smile on my face, one that I think the audience appreciates as I begin my talk.

• **Remember Why You're There**: You're in front of that room for a reason. You have a message that's important to deliver and the expertise and perspective to support that message. Don't forget that. You were invited to be there. You're there with purpose. You deserve to be there.

• **Medication**: When I recently searched online for "public speaking," terms like "medication" and "pills" showed up early in the results, illustrating the strong demand for relief from nervousness. While there are medications that can help with anxiety (and their discussion goes well beyond the scope of this book), I strongly advise against using any medication without the oversight of a medical professional. Self-medication can lead to a disastrous talk and be dangerous to your health. And I don't recommend self-medicating with alcohol. Speaking requires being sharp, and I've found that even a small amount of alcohol can take me off my game. If you do choose to medicate — whether prescribed or not — be sure to test the medicine well in advance of your speaking engagement. You don't want to find yourself having an adverse reaction or losing focus on stage. I do confess to some self-medication: I try to drink plenty of water before a talk. In the end, my hope is that any need you have for medication to control anxiety before speaking publicly will diminish over time as you grow more and more comfortable with that microphone in your hand.

Your Audience is Your Team

Myth: "Imagine That Everyone in Your Audience is Naked"

Fact: This is an absurd urban myth that simply won't die. I can't imagine anything more distracting — and disturbing! At one level it is comical, but at another, this counters everything that's true about your audience. You want to show your audience respect and engage with them...not undress them. This myth sets up an adversarial relationship between you and your audience. Your audience is your ally — they're on your side! I suppose if you're going to imagine anything, imagine them all with their hands in the air with a big thumbs up...and dressed.

A common view of public speaking is that you're standing *alone* in front of the crowd, under pressure, all eyes on you with anticipation. But what most speakers haven't considered is that they are not alone at all. All those eyes belong to people who are cheering you on. Your audience wants you to succeed, they're rooting for you. They're with you. Even those who don't agree with your message want you to make a successful speech. So warmly embrace your audience...they're your teammates.

It's Not About You

We've touched on this earlier, but it's crucial to emphasize this point. When you take your place in front of your audience, it's natural to feel that it's about you. You may feel self-conscious and uncomfortable as the center of attention. But remember — it's really not about you. It's about your message. The audience wants to hear what you have to say. So one of the most potent tools in your speaker toolbox — one that can be very effective at taming those butterflies — is to focus on your message, not on yourself. Once you immerse yourself in your words, they will guide you. Your message is important. Focus on setting it free, giving it life, making it shine, making it clear, and making it memorable.

Part IV

Visuals and Technology

"A picture is worth a thousand words, but only if you can remember what you were trying to say in the first place."

Jarod Kintz

Chapter Seven

Visuals: Your Friend and Foe

"Power corrupts. PowerPoint corrupts absolutely."

Edward Tufte

T his chapter and the two that follow could each merit a book of their own. The topics of visuals, technology and speaking virtually are complex, comprehensive and changing rapidly. I've chosen to keep these chapters succinct, presenting highlights and the most important lessons that I have learned. But there's much more that could be told, and my pen may fill the pages of future books to do so. (See *Beyond this Book*.)

Using Visuals

The Importance of Visuals and the Importance of Training to Create Them

Visuals can be vital to a presentation, especially when the content is, well, visual. Visuals can help you provide additional context, reinforce your key points and be especially helpful for visual learners in your audience. When I give presentations, I try to take my audience underwater with me, so my presentations are full of stills and videos, meant not only to emphasize points but also to inspire and engender a sense of wonder.

Most of us use PowerPoint or Keynote as the go-to software for our presentations. (For simplicity, I'll simply refer to PowerPoint.) But when those programs came into our lives, many of us didn't receive the training we needed (if any). Sure, we learned how to create a slide, place an image into a slide, insert transitions, etc., but that's simply the mechanics. Presenting visuals is also a right-brain exercise; that is, the principles of design come into play, that is, how to create professional-looking imagery that is easy to see, easy to read, and easy to understand. It's also about aesthetics — a professional presentation needs to impress visually. There are powerful tools within PowerPoint at our finger tips and they can be tempting to use — but it's better to leave many of them unused. Bizarre transitions with sound effects are one example of using these tools improperly — such transitions can take your audience out of the presentation. Taken together, all of these factors sweep us into the realm of strong PowerPoint presentation and graphic design.

I'm a Doctor, Not a Graphic Designer

While some of us do a pretty good job designing PowerPoint presentations without formal training, most of us are not graphic designers. Some of us may cut and paste good designs from online sources (hopefully with permission and/or crediting the creators). I've had a lot of practice — I began to use PowerPoint when it was first released in 1987. And I think my slides show polish and professionalism. But recently, one of my students astounded me. In addition to her work in the environmental field, she is also a graphic designer. Not only did her slides look astonishingly good, but they also brilliantly communicated their points. She's raised the bar for me. If you're not a graphic designer and feel that you need to elevate the quality of your presentation but don't feel like you have the skills (and aren't lucky enough to have someone in-house at your organization to help you), you can outsource this type of work. Sites like Upwork, Fiverr and 99designs can connect you with designers who can readily take on such tasks at an affordable price.

The Biggest PowerPoint Blunder

We've all endured it and many of us have done it (and have hopefully learned better). As briefly mentioned earlier, *PowerPoint is not a script of your speech*! It is not some sort of teleprompter from which you read your speech to your audience. How many of us have squinted at a screen, impossibly packed with bullet points so small that they can't be discerned from the front row, as the presenter reads each point? *PowerPoint should complement your speech, not dominate it.* It is a tool that allows you to visually present concepts that would otherwise be difficult to explain (such as a bar chart or infographic), or imagery, such as a beautiful octopus at the bottom of the Bering Sea. There's no rule against bullet points, but remember, your audience tends not to be able to read much text while you're speaking unless you spoon-feed a small number of words to them. (This can be aided by using the feature in PowerPoint that displays only one bullet item at a time.) Better yet, forget the bullet points and simply show images. Your spoken words are more powerful than text your audience may not read.

You Are Here

If you've put together a well-structured presentation, PowerPoint can be especially helpful at presenting the key sections of your talk, essentially a roadmap. I like to use an initial roadmap slide to show all of the sections we'll be covering, and a roadmap slide at the beginning of each section showing where we area. On those slides I still display all of the sections, but only the current section is highlighted — the others are greyed out. This approach reminds your audience of the overall structure, where you've been and where you're going. This approach helps reinforce the structure of your presentation and help your audience more clearly follow your flow of logic.

A Slide About Nothing

One of the most powerful slides you may want to incorporate in your presentation is no slide at all. In other words, a blank slide (colored black or a dark color so little or no light reaches the screen). The fact that there is no slide on the screen focuses the audience's attention back on you. This provides a dramatic pause in the presentation that allows you to emphasize a point, make other points, connect with your audience and break up the presentation.

Use Slides Sparingly (or Don't)

The conventional wisdom for visuals is to use them sparingly, and this is sound advice. Your audience is easily overwhelmed with information, and flying through a large slide deck can actually reduce your audience's comprehension and understanding. At worst, they may simply tune out. Select the key points you want to make and use slides sparingly. On the other hand, if you're someone like me, do the opposite. Since I use many visuals to illustrate my points, most without any written words, I use many slides — mostly photographs and a few videos — to help me tell a story. Event organizers are sometimes shocked when I arrive with a slide deck of 120 slides for a 40-minute presentation. But in such presentations, I see myself in the role of a narrator of a movie, so there are many slides but they are fast-paced and keep the audience's attention. Displaying a slide for five seconds may seem terribly short, but if you watch modern TV shows, movies and commercials, the cuts are even shorter. We're accustomed to fast-paced visuals and I've found it works in my case.

Integrate and Practice...Again

In Chapter 3 we discussed the importance of practicing and refining your speech. Now we need to add PowerPoint to the equation and practice and refine once more. Whether you prepare your PowerPoint slides as you craft your remarks (as I do for my classes), or create the PowerPoint slides after your remarks, in the end presenting visuals changes your presentation and the way you present it. So it's important to practice your remarks with your visuals. You may find, as I do, that your presentation evolves once your visuals are added.

PowerPoint Tech

We'll discuss some aspects of public speaking technology in the next chapter. However, I thought it best to include here several technical items specific to PowerPoint (or Keynote, etc.) If you've been a good Boy Scout, you've arrived early and have made certain everything is ready. Be sure to do a complete run-through of your presentation. Don't assume they have a copy of your presentation, even if you've sent it to them. Have it ready on a thumb drive just in case.

If you've ever seen (or given) a presentation where the fonts look missized, tables don't fit correctly, etc., it may be because you used non-standard fonts not present on a different computer (when you're not presenting from your own computer). When saving your presentation on your computer, be sure to select the option in PowerPoint to "Save Fonts" in the presentation. That way the fonts will travel with your presentation.

Because I show many videos (embedded into PowerPoint slides) in my presentations, I occasionally run into situations where, due to the size of a video, it may take several seconds for it to load. In such cases, before the presentation, I display each slide containing a video. This creates a buffer that allows the video to load more quickly the next time it is shown. Finally, I've had the unfortunate experience of my videos not playing at all on a host's computer. With apologies for the technical description, this happens principally because the host's computer does not contain the codec(s) necessary to play my videos. (A codec is a hardware- or software-based process that compresses and decompresses data, including video files.) I have found that encoding video in H.264 format (which is typically bears the suffix .mp4) provides the best compatibility. However, beware of the ancient computers. I've encountered them in schools and, most recently, a public library. Such computers may not even play your presentation because the hardware and/or software is too old (or too slow). Always have

your own computer at the ready (and use it when possible). More
on that in the next chapter.

Friend or Foe?

I consider visuals a vital tool in my presentations. And visuals
aren't limited to software slides. I like to pass around real objects,
which creates another sort of connection to your presentation.
But when it comes to PowerPoint and other presentation software,
misuse it and it can unravel an otherwise great talk. Use it wisely
and it can help elevate your words and help your audience better
understand — and appreciate — your talk.

Chapter Eight

A Fistfull of Dongles: Technology and Public Speaking

"I love technology. It provides us with new and exciting ways to complain about technology."

Matt Groening

Dealing with technology has been a thread through this book, including in the previous chapter about PowerPoint, Keynote and other presentation technology and in the next chapter on speaking virtually using Zoom, Teams and other virtual meeting software. And while there is some overlap with those chapters, I feel it's important to break technology out into its own chapter. After all, though unimaginable as we are well into the 21st century, it seems that at every meeting or conference I attend, one speaker or another encounters a technology problem. As with Chapters 7 and 9, so much more could be written about this important topic, but again, I summarize this important topic to cover the most important topics.

Earlier we discussed the critical importance of preparation, including the many questions you'll need to ask about the venue in which you are to be speaking, whether it be a massive speaking hall or in the confines of a conference room. High on the list are questions about the technology you'll be encountering.

Your Computer or Mine?

In many talks, you'll use your own laptop for your presentation. If that's the case, what will you be connecting to? A projector? An LCD panel? What cables will you need? Or will the connections be wireless? Will there be a mini headphone jack for audio (if you're playing video or music) or will sound be transmitted through an HDMI cable?

I've arrived at some venues where the hosts had no idea about the technology, just pointing me toward the podium, offering the helpful advice, "There should be something to connect to your laptop." In contrast, onstage prior to a speech I gave in South Dakota, I was swarmed by six tech-guy "commandos" in black shirts with all manner of wires, connectors and microphones and after a flurry of activity, my laptop was plugged in and ready to go.

Be prepared for some MacGyver-ing. I use a Windows PC and have arrived at Mac-only schools and organizations with Mac-only connectors that required substantial effort — and time — to change out. I arrived at a venue where the entire A/V system was locked in a cabinet and no one could produce a key. The show must go on, so I forced open (translate: broke) the door to get access and had to push all sorts of buttons to get the system to work. I can't count the number of times I've been on my knees, hanging with the dust bunnies under the tables to get things hooked up.

I've learned to bring a large assortment of connectors and dongles, spares, extension cords and dongles to be sure I can connect to the host's A/V system. After all these years, I still get stumped. I recently arrived at a school in Virginia where budget limitations meant that their PowerPoint projector was ancient and could only connect using a VGA connector, one which I hadn't countered in more than a decade. I didn't have an adapter with me. One of the teachers disappeared for 15 minutes and managed to find one, albeit with a broken pin, so my slides had an unpleasant green cast to them. Needless to say I now carry a VGA adapter with me. I can provide a checklist of recommended tech items you should bring to every presentation (see *Beyond This Book*) at the end of the book.

I've discussed timing and the user of a timer in Chapters 2 and 5. I do *not* recommend using the built-in timer function of a smartphone as your speech timer as it is limited in capabilities, the screen saver can cause the screen to go dark, and your phone may lock. I prefer to use apps designed for speech timing such as *Speech Timer for Talks* by Senzillo Inc., which costs $0.99 at the time of this writing. The criteria to look for are (1) The app stays on and the screen does not dim or go dark during its use; (2) The phone does not lock while the app is running; (3) You can set warning points as you wish. These will typically turn the color of the countdown clock's numerals from green to yellow to red. (4) The timer allows for overtime, i.e., if you go over, you can see by how much you have run over.

Some important rules I always follow when giving a presentation with my own computer:

- Never update any software before a presentation. In fact, I never update software while traveling. An unsuccessful update can wreak havoc on your computer and/or other software.

- Never give a presentation on battery power. Not only might you run out of juice, but performance is usually lackluster when running on battery. You might also receive battery power notices from the operating system, interrupting your presentation.

- If avoidable, never depend on an Internet connection for a presentation. Download videos and other materials from the Internet if you can.

- Disable your operating system's notifications and disable all non-essential programs on your computer, especially browsers, email clients, messaging and other applications that might give an intrusive pop-up message (which may contain personal information). Closing apps can also help with your computer's performance. In the past I have sometimes set up a separate profile just for giving presentations where there are a minimum number of apps loaded. At one point I even had a completely separate computer dedicated for presentations.

In the prior chapter I discussed some of the perils of using the "house computer," and sometimes you really don't know what type of technology you'll encounter until you arrive. For very large conferences I have have consulted directly with the A/V team to be sure my visuals are working correctly. (The team is often in the back of the room or sequestered into a control room or other private space.)

The bottom line: Ask questions weeks (or at least days) in advance, show up early, bring your dongles, make sure everything works, brush the dust bunnies off your knees, and enjoy a well-earned sigh of relief.

Part V

Speaking Virtually

"Zoom meetings: Where pants are optional, but awkward moments are mandatory."

Ellen DeGeneres

Chapter Nine

Learning to Speak Virtually

"Public speaking in a virtual environment is like performing on a digital stage – you have to find a way to make your audience forget they're sitting at their desks."

Julian Treasure

I have always believed in face-to-face meetings, so much so that I have traveled long distances to "be a face" at a meeting, to make that essential human connection, and hopefully a more significant and more memorable impact. So the rapid and significant movement toward virtual meetings in the post-pandemic world has been a difficult adjustment. What virtual meetings offer in convenience and significant savings of time and money they sacrifice in terms of the breadth and depth of the human connection. They also limit informal interaction. I've always felt that the magic of a conference is found in the informal hallway meetings. Those are all but absent in most formal online conferences.

The first semester I taught at Johns Hopkins University was during the pandemic. Consequently, I needed to teach a class of 18 graduate students over Zoom. At the university building from which I taught, it was a surreal experience. Only four people were in the entire building during my evening class: another professor, a security guard, a janitor and I. Teaching online took getting used to, but surprisingly, I didn't hate it. In some ways, it was a more intimate experience: I met students' pets, got a peek into their homes, and occasionally spotted a spouse carrying a laundry basket. And since I was teaching a class, I could use the breakout feature in Zoom to create small groups of students for informal discussion, at least a step toward replicating the hallway chat.

While many of us had grown accustomed over the years to speaking on conference calls, the mastery of virtual visual meetings is challenging. We're still adapting to something that is new and rapidly evolving. Speaking virtually is more challenging than it seems.

Connecting With a Virtual Audience

Virtual speaking can shortchange us of many tools we would normally consider essential to connecting to the audience. Interacting with your audience is much more constrained in a virtual setting. We've discussed the importance of moving about the stage, using gestures and arm movements and projecting a strong and dynamic presence. When speaking virtually, you're basically a talking head with very limited ability to use body language in your presentation. Maintaining eye contact with your audience has a new set of challenges. To make direct eye contact, looking as close to directly into the camera is necessary. You can't make eye contact with audience members individually. Look at an individual in a square at the bottom of the screen and you'll be seen by others as looking down and losing eye contact. To make matters worse, if you're sharing your screen to make a PowerPoint or other presentation, your face will be relegated to a tiny box where, at best, your facial expressions will be barely visible, and at worst, you'll be ignored entirely. Your stage presence in a real-world talk is far more magnified.

Speaking virtually, you may not be able to see all of your audience or perhaps none of your audience at all. (When I have guest speakers from around the world deliver their remarks to my class through Zoom, I position the webcam so it captures my entire class so that at least the guest speaker can connect with the students in a limited way.) When giving a live speech or presentation, you can make eye contact, read your audience and their reactions and make adjustments along the way. You can be more spontaneous. When speaking virtually, you're not quite flying blind, but it can be challenging to read your audience, especially if you can't see them. Not seeing your audience at all is, to me, the worst of all virtual speaking challenges. No eye contact. No signs of life. Just your webcam staring back at you.

You can compensate through strong facial expressions and use of your hands, but it can feel quite unnatural because, well, it is. No doubt this will feel more and more natural as we adapt, but at this point there remain many who are far from feeling "natural" using this form of communication. Do your best to "make eye contact" with your webcam, not your screen. I recently gave the keynote address for a major ocean conservation conference in Riyadh. At the last minute, they decided that it would be best for me to deliver my remarks virtually from Washington, DC. It was 3:30 AM my time. I was wearing a suit and tie (with shorts, of course). I saw none of the hundreds of participants on my screen and spoke into the tiny lens of my webcam for 40 minutes. I found it a difficult speech to give. I was in the blind. I couldn't tell if the connection was solid or if they had been disconnected minutes earlier. (Fortunately, the Internet gods cooperated.) But speaking to an inanimate object in the middle of the night was a very unnatural experience. Some colleagues, when called upon to deliver a virtual speech, have assembled a small live audience, making it feel more natural. Such a hybrid meeting may require different technology (and pants) and the speaker needs to remember to make eye contact with the camera, not just their live audience.

When giving talks or participating in meetings, many participants disable their cameras. I like to think they're just having a bad hair day, but for all I know, they've gone shopping. A live audience is undoubtedly subject to distraction(e.g., checking smartphones, having conversations). In virtual meetings, distractions are amplified dramatically when participants may be getting their kids ready for bed, making dinner, running through an airport, or, for those seated in front of the computer, working or surfing the web while they listen. It can be a tremendous challenge for the speaker to rise above such distractions and command the audience's attention.

Fortunately, many of the basics of public speaking we've discussed apply to speaking virtually. A strong speech, well-crafted, well-delivered and well-timed, can surmount many of the challenges of delivering a speech virtually. However, I've found that I've had to find new ways to keep my students and other virtual audiences engaged. The use of polls, chat and breakout groups can be very effective tools. Breaking the audience into small groups to discuss specific topics and having a group representative report back to the larger group can keep your audience engaged. I've also found that instructing the audience to place questions into the chat window of Zoom, Teams, etc. is another good way to keep a presentation interactive. You'll need to allocate more time for breakout groups and Q&A via chat, meaning you'll likely need to shorten your remarks as compared to giving a live speech.

I've discovered that real-time polling and quiz apps (Slido and Kahoot are two popular examples) can be fun and engaging. We've had lots of fun with such competitions in my classes. (Several smartphone apps allow you to create competitive quizzes, keeping score and replete with fun graphics and a leader board. The participants download the app and respond on their smartphones.)

Look the Part and Sound Even Better

Now Hear This

In virtual meetings, conferences and even television interviews, the most neglected element — yet the most important — is audio. If you can't be understood your audience will miss your important content and possibly become annoyed and/or tune out. I advise against relying on a laptop, webcam or mobile phone's built-in microphone or the microphones of earbuds, to pick up and broadcast your voice. The sound is often mediocre, prone to echo (sounding like you're speaking from inside a tin can) and, at times, nearly impossible to understand. If you use a mobile device (phone or tablet), there are inexpensive wireless microphones that plug into your device and wirelessly (via Bluetooth) communicate with an included lapel microphone. I always carry such a setup with me — it fits into a small case about twice the size of an earbud case. For my laptop or desktop computer, I always use a fairly large external microphone and sometimes lug it with me for important calls where I will be using my laptop. Headphones with a boom microphone are also a good option, but not a professional look if you're delivering a speech. Again, I strongly recommend not relying on the built-in microphones of your laptop, webcam, smartphone or earbuds.

Dress the Set

Visually, we're not ready for prime time. (Even some commentators speaking from their homes on TV during prime time aren't ready for prime time.) Looking professional — or even being visible at all — requires "dressing the set." Lighting is the most important factor in determining the quality of your appearance, even more important than the "set" itself. You may have seen meeting participants appear in so much in shadow that they appear as a silhouette (and may disappear altogether when the sun goes down). Conversely, you may have seen speakers whose face is brightly lit but the background is completely dark, making them appear as a spooky, disembodied head. And speaking of spooky, sitting under typical office fluorescent lights can cast unflattering — if not ghoulish — shadows on one's face.

I always use external lighting — inexpensive LED lighting with simple controls to change the light's temperature and intensity. Some of these can clip on to your computer or other object or can stand freely. I recommend always using such lighting to fill unflattering shadows. Avoid lighting your face directly (that is, placing the light directly in front of your face). In addition to being blinding, the light will be very flat and unflattering, often washing out the definition of your features. I place my light at an angle of roughly 20-40 degrees. This casts a small but flattering shadow that brings out the definition of my face. These lights, usually rechargeable, easily fit in your backpack or briefcase and I always carry one with me.

Now back to the disembodied head. Always be sure to light the "set" behind you. You'll need to experiment with this, but even with a blurred background it can make a world of difference. Avoid having a window directly behind you. Bright light can adversely affect the image and result in your face being silhouetted against bright background light.

Finally, anticipate changing light conditions. I speak from my desk, which is beside a window. As the sun sets, I adjust my lighting accordingly. Zoom and other software will compensate for low light conditions, but the results can be unpredictable. I prefer to have control.

Set Design

We've all been thrust into a world where our living room may be broadcast to all corners of the globe. Many of us have space constraints and may not have an ideal place for a "Zoom set." In general, remember, you're the star, not your setting. Make it simple and tidy but do avoid putting yourself in front of a sterile blank white wall. Don't show off your swimming medals or latest book. If you choose a virtual background, a green screen is a worthwhile investment if you are frequently speaking virtually as the quality of virtual background effect is far superior to that processed natively by Zoom, Teams, etc.

It's About You, Not Your Nose

Take time to position your webcam at a flattering height. For many laptops, the angle of the built-in webcam is such that your audience may be looking up your nose (and you'll appear to be looking down on them (and no one likes to be looked down upon). Take the time to place your laptop on a stable object where the height is more natural. (I travel with a light,collapsible laptop stand.) The same is true for your smartphone or other mobile devices. For those I invested in an inexpensive stand that sits stably upon a desk and also telescopes so that I can use it while standing. Combined with my portable lighting and wireless lapel mike, my iPhone makes for a great Zoom studio while on the go.

No Sweats

If you're asked to speak virtually, or even if you're just a participant in a meeting, you don't get a pass for appearance just because it's a virtual meeting. Many working from home have grown accustomed to sweatpants and torn t-shirts, but they have no place in a meeting. It shouldn't need to be said, but dress professionally and don't forget to groom thyself.

Lying Down on the Job

During a recent Zoom call, I was taken aback by one participant leaning back on his couch — way back — and barely making eye contact with the camera. At a certain point I was sure he was asleep. Please remember — it may be virtual, but it's still a meeting. Sit up straight and conduct yourself as you would at an in-person meeting. Don't stuff your face with a hoagie until after the meeting. It comes back to respecting your audience.

You're Muted

Prepare for a virtual speech with the same "Boy Scout" preparation you would in a non-virtual address. I prepare an hour in advance, hoping I only need five minutes. On occasion, however, I've needed the full hour. Like an in-person speech, a virtual speech depends upon technology. The stakes are higher than when giving a live speech. If you can't get Zoom to work, you're pretty much dead in the water. So in addition to many of the preparation steps you would make for an in-person speech (such as confirming the time, introductions, etc.), speaking virtually requires its own unique set of preparation steps, mostly oriented toward technology:

- Be sure your hardware and software are working. On occasion, I've been stymied by a required update by Zoom that costs me valuable time.

- Run through the software — there may be changes. Online meeting software is evolving quickly, meaning that the user interface can change without warning. Be sure you are familiar with the latest version of the software. You don't want to hear those dreaded words, "You're muted."

- Make sure your sound, lighting and set are prepared.

- Test your audio and video and make necessary adjustments.

- Be sure your Internet connection is strong. This is especially important if you're in a location you're not familiar with.

- Be sure your set is tidy and quiet. I take the view that pets are allowed (my cat adores Zoom meetings) but that's a matter I'll leave to you.

- If you're in an unfamiliar location, check to see if there will be any unexpected interruptions, like a mass of students passing through. The events director at the Free Library of Philadelphia was kind enough to allow me to stay after a speech to give a television interview from one of the conference rooms. There was a catch, however. We discovered that the lights would automatically shut off if the room's sensors did not detect movement in the room. Thankfully, my brother meandered about the conference room until my interview was completed.

- Now that we so commonly deliver talks across the world, be sure to check and double-check time zones.

- Don't lose the meeting link! Copy and paste it into your calendar so you don't need to pore through hundreds of emails to locate it at the very last minute.

Looking Ahead

Virtual meetings appear to be here to stay and they will continue to evolve. More and more we're also seeing hybrid meetings — incorporating both live and virtual participants. This comes with a new set of challenges for the speaker. Again, in the end, the fundamentals of public speaking will always serve you well, whatever the technology. And your audience is still part of your team, even if you never see them.

Part VI

From Competent to Captivating

"The only source of knowledge is experience."

Albert Einstein

Chapter Ten

Becoming a Captivating Speaker

"Connecting with the audience is not about what you say, but how you make them feel."

Michael H. Mescon

Advancing From Competent to Captivating

E levating yourself from a competent speaker to a captivating speaker isn't magic or complicated — it simply builds upon the basic elements we have already discussed. That means if you've made it this far, you've already completed the bulk of the work and are probably already standing apart from other speakers. This chapter largely builds on what we've learned so far while also introducing several new concepts.

Elevating Your Connection

Earlier we discussed the importance of authenticity, engaging and inspiring your audience. This is especially important for motivational speakers but applies equally to sales presentations and training sessions. In sales, it's easy for a prospect to say "no" to buying a product. It's harder to say "no" to a person you've connected with.

You want your audience to connect with you and feel your interest, enthusiasm and passion about the subject. Your delivery — even if in the more formal "oratory" genre where the speaker can come across as distant from the audience — can benefit greatly from a conversational element, something that can be very effective in reducing the distance between you and your audience. Eye contact is essential. Lock eyes with various members of the audience. It can help them feel special and more engaged while helping *you* recognize that they are in this with you, part of your team. Your authenticity, passion, enthusiasm and sincerity will resonate with your audience, capture their attention, make you more relatable and take your connection to another level. Your passion engenders theirs, even if the topic isn't one they know well or care about.

An example: How about the love of slimy things of the deep, like fish. (Once again, please indulge this marine scientist.) As one who has dedicated much of his life to ocean conservation, I see fish more as friends rather than food. So on occasion, I'll pause my PowerPoint presentation on a slide of a magnificent red hind grouper (Google it — it's a beautiful fish — well, to me anyway). I show a closeup I took of him, facing the camera. I sometimes walk over and face the screen, throw my arms up and shout, "Look at that beautiful face!" It's a bit silly but has a touch of humor and authenticity that the audience seems to enjoy. They might not leave the venue loving a red hind grouper quite the way I do, but I've hopefully imparted a passion that will stay with them. Expressing such emotion can feel uncomfortable at first but comes naturally with practice and your increasing comfort in front of an audience.

Building a connection with your audience is a two-way process — often a two-way dialogue. When crafting your remarks you did your research about your audience. During the speech, be attentive, responsive, and adaptive to your audience's reactions and needs. Even if it means going off script, this strengthens your connection. Below I discuss *The Importance of Empathy* which includes many of the same elements.

One important point to remember when connecting with your audience. People tend to be shy and reserved in a crowd. You may ask a question of your audience (see *The Curious Power of Curiosity* below) and the sound of crickets fills the room. As we discussed earlier, a short pause can seem like an hour, but wait long enough and someone is bound to raise their hand. If not, it can make you uncomfortable, but don't sweat it. It doesn't mean they're not interested — it can simply mean they're shy or afraid of providing the wrong answer. The same goes for the curious silence that might come when you're sure the audience will laugh at part of your presentation you were sure would get belly laughs. Unfortunately, audiences just don't understand when they're supposed to laugh. (And recall my story of speaking at the parochial school where the students might be reprimanded if they did laugh.) Don't be daunted — it's natural for audiences to be reserved.

Authenticity

Elevating your connection with your audience demands your authenticity and your sincerity. You want the audience to connect with the "real" you. This isn't always an easy task. At one level, a public speech is bigger than life — a performance of sorts — requiring you to deliver your words with more drama and volume than you would at the dinner table. But at the same time, your speech isn't a Broadway show. You're not an actor playing a part. You're you being you, but a more animated you, and sometimes perhaps a more "dramatic" version of yourself. (Many of the great comedians share personal stories and a bit of themselves along the way. Exaggerated? Undoubtedly. But they allow some of their real personality to shine through.) But don't force it. If it doesn't feel right in your gut, don't go there. The key is to cling to your authenticity, and that's what elevates your connection. Your audience wants to connect to *you*, and they can tell if you're forcing it. Be yourself and you'll draw your audience close.

You may have heard speakers, say at a training seminar, who do everything right that we talked about in Chapter 5: Their eye contact is impeccable, their eloquent delivery is completely devoid of "ums," their posture is tall and confident, they have strong stage presence, their voice projects to the back of the room, etc. They're bigger than life, often funny as hell, and successful at keeping your attention. But in the end, it seems more of an act, their role being one of a performer. Although the public-speaking primordial soup is rich with all of the necessary ingredients, the connection is missing or seems contrived and inauthentic. In fairness, many of these trainers have obviously given the same presentation and told the same jokes hundreds of times, but their speaking style gets the job done. In contrast, I've attended other training sessions where the trainer allows themself to be more authentic, by relating certain elements of the training to their own experiences for example. In turn, this fosters a better sense of who the trainer is, and engenders a greater sense of authenticity and a strong connection. With rare exception, those are the trainers I remember.

What about prepared statements? Often we witness spokespersons from law enforcement, governmental agencies, the military, corporations and other entities reading prepared statements. Such statements are carefully crafted in a generalized way so as not to reveal too much specific information and scrupulously navigate politically charged waters. Therefore, in most cases, the spokesperson must read such statements verbatim. Typically, a sheriff's public statement on, say, a shooting, is read in an especially dry and robotic manner — devoid of emotion. (This is similar to the experience I shared in Chapter 2 of a commencement I attended where the university official read a speech of beautifully written words without emotion, in an uninspiring monotone, with no eye contact with the audience, robbing that ceremony of the inspiration and emotional impact it deserved.)

Even with the constraints of a prepared statement, one can, through authentic and emotive expression, move beyond the rote recitation of an official statement without deviating from the script or sacrificing authority. I was impressed to see an official briefing to the public on CNN about a tragic shooting, but the law enforcement official expressed his sincere emotion and empathy for the victims even as he read verbatim from a prepared statement. His briefing had a strong impact on me. Conveying his sincere emotion told me that he and his law enforcement colleagues were impacted by the seriousness of the crime, its toll on the victims, and, in turn, how committed they were to track down and capture the suspect. That is the one briefing I remember the most in, sadly, a plethora of such briefings in recent times.

Speak to the Heart

We're human, and as such, respond strongly to emotion, more so than a list of facts, and we are wired to remember emotional events in our lives. As aptly put in an article in the journal *Nature*,

"Emotional events often attain a privileged status in memory" (LaBar and Cabeza, 2006).

My approach to speaking and teaching follows the adage "Speak to the heart and the mind will soon follow." Through underwater images and video of the beauty and wonder of the undersea world, I've hopefully imparted an emotional response. I find such an approach draws the audience in. Had I presented bullet points on the volume and depth of the ocean, I suspect the response would be much different. Eventually, I do address some of those statistics, but not without first touching the heart by fostering a sense of wonder, imagination and curiosity.

I'm very fortunate to have a topic — the oceans — that lends itself to presentations that naturally create an emotional response. What if you're training a class on the repair of a diesel engine? One approach night be to include anecdotes involving such engines and the importance of keeping them in impeccable condition. Even better — a personal experience, like the time the Cummins engine in the Peterbilt you were driving seized up on I-95 in a blizzard. (I really hope that didn't happen to anyone.)

The Importance of Empathy

In Chapter 2 we discussed the importance of knowing your audience — who are they, what do they know and what do they need? Taking your speaking to a higher level includes not only understanding the needs and interests of your audience, but beyond that to be able to express empathy for their concerns, fears, or aspirations. Your empathy allows you to connect on an emotional level, showing genuine care and appreciation. At a water quality conference in Canada, I singled out the unsung workers at some of the water treatment plants and the hard work they are facing, especially with climate change causing more storms, bringing their plants to capacity with much more water to process. The brief comment helped those workers feel recognized at a time that they were under duress, and it was appreciated by the rest of the audience as well.

What if I Cry?

At a recent conference, one of the presenters was in the middle of a powerful and emotional presentation when she broke down and cried. As an audience member, I felt empathetic but, I suppose like many other audience members, I also felt uncomfortable...I wanted to know if she was OK. In short order, the speaker regained her composure and completed her speech. Her audience loudly applauded, responding to the content of her remarks and the depth of the sincerity and emotion with which she conveyed it.

I sometimes tear up a bit when I'm teaching — occasionally just by imagery of the ocean that I find overwhelmingly beautiful. Our natural instinct is to feel embarrassment if we cry in front of our audience. Speakers invariably apologize to the audience as if crying conveys weakness. I argue the opposite. We're humans.

We feel. Expressing emotion — even crying — is something that clearly shows the depth of how much we care and connect to the topic we're presenting. First, let the audience know you're OK to relieve their concern that you're not having a serious breakdown. We all have different ways of doing this. Nodding, eeking out, "I'm OK," a quick smile, placing your hand on your heart, etc. It's not obligatory but can bring some comfort to your audience.

And don't apologize. It's common, and it's polite, but it's entirely unnecessary. You've done something positive and powerful for your audience — you've shared your emotional connection to the issue you're presenting. I have broken into tears in front of an audience of hundreds. Once I regained my composure, I told the audience that I obviously was very emotionally invested in the issue (or something of that nature). Remember, the courage to share your emotions is a human strength, not a weakness.

The Power of Storytelling

When a speaker tries to make a point by reading bullet point after bullet point on a PowerPoint slide, most of us tune out. (I tend to scream inside my head.) In contrast, telling a story that illustrates your points can be far more powerful...and interesting. Sharing personal stories, anecdotes, or experiences can engender a sense of relatability and authenticity. Such stories allow the audience to connect with you on a more personal level, and they can be used to evoke emotions in the process of illustrating your points.

There's a growing body of brain science offering insight explaining how differently our brains process stories and why our attention is significantly increased when we listen to a story rather than a recitation of facts. In one study, neuroscience researchers found that during storytelling, the brainwaves of the storyteller and the listener actually began to "synchronize," improving the listener's attentiveness and comprehension. (Stephens *et al.*, 2010). Recall in Chapter 2 my Everglades speech that begin with a story of a church in the Soviet Union. The unusual story drew my audience in, setting the stage for the remainder of my talk.

It's common for speakers to "write themselves into the script," i.e., telling personal stories of their own lives and experiences. Our personal stories can go a long way to connect with our audience and convey our authenticity. But sharing of one's self through storytelling has its challenges. One needs to be careful of "oversharing" and consequently making your presentation too personal. At the extreme, you can stray into the level of telling a "cringe-worthy" story which, in turn, can create an awkward connection with your audience by making them feel uncomfortable. I've also seen personal storytelling used as a crutch for an unprepared speech, where speakers drone on with unprepared personal stories well past their time limit. In such cases, their stories can come across as self-indulgent and/or boastful.

The Curious Power of Curiosity

We *Homo sapiens* are naturally curious beasts. Hand-in-hand with storytelling is curiosity, something inevitably woven into the fabric of a story. It can significantly further the potency of your story. Curiosity can also stand on its own, a great way to introduce a topic or story. Ask the audience a question. It piques their curiosity and draws them in. Teachers know this instinctively. In one presentation I'll ask audience members to close their eyes and listen. I darken the room with only a deep, dark blue slide on the screen — it sets a delicious, spooky ambiance. I then play an audio clip that sounds absolutely unworldly. I ask the audience if they know what sea creature they just heard. Most guess it's a whale or dolphin, but it's not. Invariably they're stumped — I have their attention because I've dramatically piqued their curiosity. (Are you curious about what it is? See...it works! See the *Beyond this Book* section and I'll guide you to a link so you can hear this amazing sound and meet the culprit responsible.)

Woven into the stories I share with middle-school students are many opportunities to pique their curiosity in the same way. I like to introduce them to the deep ocean by sharing my experiences as a submersible pilot, showing video of taking the craft down to 2,000 feet. On the descent, at about 900 feet, my sub was being "attacked" by hundreds of large squid, squirting ink and grabbing onto the sub in what appeared to be a very aggressive manner. There are oohs and aahs and laughter. The video naturally sparks their curiosity, opening the door for me to ask the obvious question: "Why were they attacking my sub?" The students eagerly shout out their theories. With the students on the edge of their seats, it sets the stage for me to explain how squid are attracted to light (by the lights on the sub in this case), because their natural prey are bioluminescent fish. The squid were essentially trying to eat the sub — the biggest bioluminescent fish they've ever seen! (More laughter.) With the students' curiosity engaged, I go on to explain how dark the deep ocean is, how many deep-sea creatures are bioluminescent, emitting flashes of light in the dark to attract a mate, etc. Whatever your profession and field of specialization, there are stories to tell, funny, sad, mysterious or enlightening. Tap into your audience's curiosity. Challenge their imagination. Take them on a journey!

Elevating Your Delivery

It's Not About You

Focusing on your message — and not yourself — not only helps your nervousness as previously discussed, but will also bring energy and passion to your message. Your audience will respond to your intensity, making your message more impactful. As you speak, give your message the attention and passion it deserves.

It's All About You

While it's true that focusing on your message is an essential element of a great speech, it's also true that you're not simply a mouth and a microphone. You're not just delivering your message — you're also delivering yourself. Your delivery, your emotion and your connection make that message come alive. You are part of the message you're presenting.

Don't Dumb it Down

As you know from Chapter 2, I feel very strongly about not "dumbing down" the content you present. Becoming a captivating speaker puts forth the challenge of making your message understandable without over-diluting the content to the point of being condescending. This is truly challenging. I'm a scientist and was accustomed to speaking with and to other scientists. I had to change completely the way I communicated because my audience changed completely — I came to speak to a range of audiences, including the general public. You'll find that your audience enjoys being challenged and learning new things. Tracy Brower, a Ph.D. sociologist, citing numerous scientific studies, discusses in *Forbes* how an important "pathway toward happiness is learning" (Brower, 2021). Humans love to learn! Don't deny your audience that pleasure, especially if what you're teaching is challenging. The burden is on you, their teacher, to help them understand and experience the joy of learning.

R-E-S-P-E-C-T

A captivating speaker successfully orchestrates the many elements we've discussed and does so in a way that shows respect for the audience. You've prepared well, completed your research about the audience's interests and needs, responded to those needs, connected and engaged with them, challenged your audience, didn't dumb down your material, perhaps shared a story or two, piqued their curiosity, responded to their feedback, honored your time allocation, paid attention to protocol, expressed humility, and offered your gratitude. And, of course, you've embraced your audience as your ally, not your adversary. As a result, your audience will reciprocate with their respect for you.

Am I Captivating Yet?

It's a fair question. At what point can consider yourself a captivating speaker? The answer is, of course, subjective (and really, so is the word "captivating"). In the *Preface* I said that in my experience, it's a speaker people will remember, when an individual has made a strong, often emotional impact on their audience — no matter what the subject — and someone who demonstrates confidence and warmly embraces their audience with respect.

Judgment ultimately rests both with your audience and you. As for audience members, peers, etc., compliments and congratulations are good signs that you've crossed beyond competent to a higher level of public speaking proficiency. Seeing that you've left an emotional impact on your audience is another sign. And being a memorable speaker — where someone may say that they remember you speaking at a particular event years prior — is another good sign. Part of the answer rests with you. Have you tamed your butterflies? Do you feel more confident than before? Has your connection with your audience reached a new level? In my case, I gradually felt these things and one day realized that I might actually have become a good speaker – perhaps even better than good. In the end, becoming a strong public speaker isn't represented by a distinct finish line. Rather, it's a lifelong journey, one that requires commitment, hard work and ongoing self-improvement. Along that journey, you'll come to realize that you have indeed taken yourself to a higher level to become an impactful and memorable speaker — a speaker who is indeed captivating.

Epilogue

B efore you purchased this book, you no doubt came to the conclusion that becoming a better speaker is important to your career, academic pursuits, or aspect of your life. Quality public speaking is an essential part of our society, yet surprisingly, many of us have arrived at the point of our life where we need to speak publicly but have had precious little training for such an important skill.

You would think there would be a strong push for more public speaking education in our schools. In fact, in the U.S. there is a strong push, but in the opposite direction. *The Atlantic* article reports growing resistance to some forms of public speaking education in U.S. schools. Some students say having to speak in front of the class is an unreasonable burden for those with anxiety and are demanding alternative options. Citing a 2018 study by the Association of American Colleges and Universities, *The Atlantic* states that "oral communication is one of the most sought-after skills in the workplace, with over 90 percent of hiring managers saying it's important. Some educators also credit in-class presentations with building essential leadership skills and increasing students' confidence and understanding of material." Nevertheless, delivering an in-class presentation, long considered a "rite of passage" for students and credited with improving public speaking skills, is now under attack as being "discriminatory to those with anxiety" with students demanding that teachers offer alternative options (Lorenz, 2018).

Again, as I discussed in the *Preface*, I do not overlook the fact that there are individuals that can have a strong, adverse emotional reaction to public speaking, beyond that of most people. For those individuals, such an experience can go as far as being traumatic. But I built the foundation of this book on my belief that most — with training and experience — can manage their fear, build confidence and become exceptional public speakers. So it concerns me to read that public speaking education in the U.S. could be vulnerable. I require the graduate students I teach to lead a class discussion. At the graduate level, many of my students are professionals, some well into their careers, yet haven't had training or many opportunities to speak publicly, let alone facilitate discussion. It is a valuable learning experience. And that's the central point of this book. You'll recall Myth #1, "Great public speakers are born, not made." In fact, public speaking skills can be learned, developed, and improved with practice and training. It is indeed a lifelong journey, but a journey of reward and fulfillment.

Beyond This Book

"Opportunities are usually disguised as hard work, so most people don't recognize them."

Ann Landers

One book can't possibly cover all of the dimensions of public speaking (which is why I plan to release additional books in this series). As you move beyond the pages of this book I encourage you to find other books and other authors who may offer different perspectives. However, reading books is one thing. Putting theory into practice is paramount. Below are some recommendations and resources that can help you put in motion the concepts we've discussed.

Speaking Clubs

Toastmasters International

https://www.toastmasters.org/

I consider Toastmasters International — in simple a public speaking club — the most helpful resource in my own journey toward improving my public speaking abilities and confidence (see Chapter 1). There is no substitute for speaking to a live audience. Toastmasters International provides that and much more, including honest and constructive feedback you almost never receive from your peers. Toastmasters International, founded in 1924, has 14,200 clubs in 148 countries with more than 270,000 members worldwide, so chances are there is a club near you. The organization is a nonprofit educational organization that "builds confidence and teaches public speaking skills." Toastmasters International provides a supportive environment where its "members prepare and deliver speeches and give and receive constructive feedback." (Toastmasters International, 2023).

Rostrum

https://www.rostrum.com.au

Rostrum is another public speaking organization founded in Australia, with over 100 clubs nationwide in that country. This organization's goal is to help individuals to become better communicators. The general format is similar to Toastmasters International. At meetings, speakers gain experience and skills in presenting speeches and receiving feedback as well as providing feedback for other speakers. Professional speaking trainers also attend meetings. Rostrum also offers an online club for members.

Speaking Classes, Workshops and Seminars

Public Speaking Classes

Community colleges and other educational organizations offer classes in public speaking. The format is often similar to Toastmasters International and Rostrum though the class duration is limited whereas you may stay a member of a speaking club indefinitely. You'll also find the cost of a speaking club far less than speaking classes.

Storytelling Classes

We've discussed the importance of storytelling as an element of public speaking, and you can help develop those skills by taking storytelling classes. These classes focus both on the writing and telling of stories. There are many different types of storytelling classes — some specific to certain genres, i.e., focused on storytelling proper versus storytelling as an element of a broader speech. Still, it's a skill very worthwhile developing, so even if you end up telling a story about dragons in your class, it can help your public speaking abilities in delivering a talk on health care by giving you practice in front of an audience, writing a clear, well-structured talk, nailing your time allotment, etc.

Learning Online

As you might expect, there are more and more opportunities to learn online, with "synchronous" classes (i.e., live and generally two-way) offered over Zoom, Teams, etc. and "asynchronous" training, such as pre-recorded lectures. Like a book, such courses can be very helpful, especially in being able to see examples of different speakers in action. However, in terms of practice, without a live audience they are limiting and best as a resource for speaking virtually.

Just Say "Yes"

There are many opportunities for public speaking that can land at our feet. Grab 'em! They can be little things, for example, your boss may ask, "Can someone run downstairs and tell the group about the change in the agenda for the rest of the week?" Raise your hand...it's a 3-5 minute "speech" under your belt! Perhaps someone called in sick who was to present to a group of volunteers. Step up. Make a toast at a dinner event. (Just be sure you haven't had too much to drink!) You can put your speaking skills to work in all of these cases. Remember though, simply because a speech might be impromptu doesn't mean you don't prepare — even mentally and quite possibly hurriedly – to structure your remarks, deliver them confidently and clearly, connect with your audience, stick to a set time frame, etc.

Some Helpful Resources From Me

If you have found this book helpful, I'd like to provide you with some additional resources that I think you would find valuable. Visit https://beabetterpublicspeaker.com/captivating or use the QR code below to receive these resources at no charge:

- **A Live Speech Preparation Checklist**, listing the details you need to review, the questions you need to ask and the preparation you need to make before you take the stage.

- **A Virtual Speech Preparation Checklist**, providing you with each step in preparing for a successful virtual speech.

- **A Presentation Technology Checklist**, providing you with the questions you'll need to ask in advance regarding technology, venue preparation, etc.

- **A Technology "Go Bag" Checklist**, with recommendations for what everyone should carry in their technology "go bag" to every presentation, dongles and all.

- **A PowerPoint Template**, to keep your audience clear about where you are in your talk, that, between each major section of your talk, provides the audience with an overview of the sections you've covered, the current section and those to be covered.

- **A Fifteen Percent Discount on a Speech.** If you invite me to speak at your venue (whether the topic is ocean exploration, public speaking, etc.) I'll provide a 15 percent discount on my honorarium. **In addition, I will donate a second speech to a local school in your/your organization's name**.

- **A Newsletter** (optional) providing ongoing public speaking advice, alerts for my upcoming speeches and books.

- **An Opportunity to Join My Review Team**: An opportunity to be part of my **Review Team** for my future books, meaning that you'll receive an **Advanced Reader Copy** (ARC) at no cost in exchange for an honest review and your feedback.

- **The Other-Worldly Sound**: And, what you've been waiting for, I'll provide you with a recording of the other-worldly underwater sound mentioned in Chapter 10 and show you the creature responsible for making it!

https://beabetterpublicspeaker.com/captivating

Your Review Greatly Matters

I would be *deeply grateful* if you could take a minute to provide your honest review of this book. In addition to the valuable feedback you can provide, it will help others find this book and benefit from its content. My profound thanks. Visit https://beabetterp ublicspeaker.com/captivating-review or use the QR code below:

https://beabetterpublicspeaker.com/captivating-review

About the Author

D r. David E. Guggenheim is an accomplished public speaker, award-winning author, educator, marine scientist, conservation leader, ocean explorer, and submersible pilot. He is the founder and president of the Washington, DC-based nonprofit organization, Ocean Doctor, dedicated to advancing the conservation of the world's oceans through scientific research, education and community engagement. He is also an Adjunct Professor at Johns Hopkins University – Advanced Academic Programs where he teaches Ocean Stewardship and Sustainability. Guggenheim has a fervent commitment to environmental education and is journeying to all 50 U.S. states to educate K-12 students about the oceans, conservation and careers in science.

As an accomplished public speaker, he is frequently invited as keynote speaker at major national and international conferences, events for nonprofit organizations, corporate events, industry associations, schools and universities, and governmental organizations and lecturer aboard cruise ships. He has testified before the U.S. Congress as well as international governmental bodies, including the United Nations and the Scottish Parliament. He is frequently in the media and has appeared on *60 Minutes, PBS Newshour,* ABC's *Good Morning America,* CNN, MSNBC, NewsNation and NPR, as well as in several documentary films and in the *New York Times.*

Guggenheim has worked in Cuba for more than 20 years leading collaborative research and conservation efforts in Cuba focused on coral reef ecosystems. His book, *The Remarkable Reefs of Cuba: Hopeful Stories from the Ocean Doctor,* is Gold Winner of the Non-Fiction Book Awards 2023 from the Non-Fiction Authors Association and details his two decades of experiences in Cuba, working in collaboration with Cuban scientists to explore that country's unique underwater ecosystems.

As an ocean explorer, Guggenheim piloted the first manned submersible dives up to 2,000 feet into the world's largest underwater canyons located in Alaska's Bering Sea. He was inducted into the Explorers Club as a National Fellow in 2008. His 2013 documentary, *Disaster at Nightingale,* details a disastrous oil spill in a remote island group in the South Atlantic that killed thousands of penguins. In addition to his conservation work, Guggenheim is an award-winning professional photographer. His work ranges from underwater wildlife to fine art studio photography, fashion and portraiture, spanning the Antarctic, the Falkland Islands/Malvinas, Cuba, Alaska, Russia, the Middle East and beyond.

Guggenheim previously served as Vice President at Ocean Conservancy, President & CEO of the Conservancy of Southwest Florida, Co-Chair of the Everglades Coalition, President of the Friends of Channel Islands National Park and Chairman of the Board of the Great Whale Conservancy. He holds a Ph.D. in Environmental Science and Public Policy from George Mason University in Virginia, a Master's in Aquatic and Population Biology from the University of California, Santa Barbara, and a Master's in Regional Science and Bachelor's in Environmental Studies from the University of Pennsylvania.

Also By the Author:

Guggenheim, D.E. (2022). *The Remarkable Reefs of Cuba: Hopeful Stories From the Ocean Doctor*. Prometheus Books. (Visit https://remarkablereefs.com or use the QR code below.)

https://remarkablereefs.com

Bibliography

Bellever Books. (2022). *Fiction Writing 101: Tips, Tricks and Exercises to Guide Beginners in Fiction Writing.*

Bower, Tracy. (2021). "Learning Is A Sure Path To Happiness: Science Proves It." *Forbes.*

Grice, Andrew. (August 28, 2014). "Old boy's club still dominates public life, according to major new report." *Independent.*

LaBar, K., Cabeza, R. "Cognitive neuroscience of emotional memory." *Nat Rev Neurosci* 7, 54–64 (2006). https://doi.org/10.1038/nrn1825

Lorenz, Taylor. (September 12, 2018). "Teens Are Protesting In-Class Presentations." *The Atlantic.*

Mercer, Neil, Ayesha Ahmed and Paul Warwick. (October 4, 2014). "We should be teaching kids public speaking in school." *Washington Post.*

Robert, General Henry M., Sarah Corbin Robert, Henry M. Robert III, William J. Evans, Daniel H. Honemann, Thomas J.

Balch, Daniel E. Seabold, and Shmuel Gerber. (2020). *Roberts Rules of Order*. PublicAffairs, an imprint of Perseus Books LLC, a subsidiary of Hachette Book Group.

Smith, D., Schlaepfer, P., Major, K. *et al*. "Cooperation and the evolution of hunter-gatherer storytelling." *Nat Commun* 8, 1853 (2017). https://doi.org/10.1038/s41467-017-02036-8

Stephens, G. J., Silbert, L. J., & Hasson, U. (2010). "Speaker–listener neural coupling underlies successful communication." *Proceedings of the National Academy of Sciences*, 107(32), 14425-14430. https://doi.org/10.1073/pnas.1008662107

Made in United States
Orlando, FL
27 January 2024

42982511R00121